pedagogical
encounters

Complicated Conversation

A Book Series of
Curriculum Studies

William F. Pinar
General Editor

VOLUME 33

PETER LANG
New York • Washington, D.C./Baltimore • Bern
Frankfurt am Main • Berlin • Brussels • Vienna • Oxford

pedagogical *encounters*

EDITED BY
Bronwyn Davies & Susanne Gannon

WITH
Catherine Camden Pratt, Constance Ellwood,
Katerina Zabrodska, & Peter Bansel

PETER LANG
New York • Washington, D.C./Baltimore • Bern
Frankfurt am Main • Berlin • Brussels • Vienna • Oxford

Library of Congress Cataloging-in-Publication Data
Pedagogical encounters / edited by Bronwyn Davies, Susanne Gannon.
p. cm. — (Complicated conversation: a book series of curriculum studies; vol. 33)
Includes bibliographical references and index.
1. Education—Philosophy. 2. Education—Australia. 3. Deleuze, Gilles,
1925–1995. I. Davies, Bronwyn. II. Gannon, Susanne.
LB14.7.P435   370.1—dc22   2009026610
ISBN 978-1-4331-0817-4 (hardcover)
ISBN 978-1-4331-0816-7 (paperback)
ISSN 1534-2816

Bibliographic information published by **Die Deutsche Nationalbibliothek**.
Die Deutsche Nationalbibliothek lists this publication in the "Deutsche
Nationalbibliografie"; detailed bibliographic data are available
on the Internet at http://dnb.d-nb.de/.

Cover photograph by Constance Ellwood
Author photo by Katerina Zabrodska

© 2009, 2016 Peter Lang Publishing, Inc., New York
29 Broadway, 18th floor, New York, NY 10006
www.peterlang.com

All rights reserved.
Reprint or reproduction, even partially, in all forms such as microfilm,
xerography, microfiche, microcard, and offset strictly prohibited.

Contents

ACKNOWLEDGMENTS vii

INTRODUCTION 1
    Bronwyn Davies

CHAPTER 1 17
    DIFFERENCE AND DIFFERENCIATION
    Bronwyn Davies

CHAPTER 2 31
    LISTENING TO HOMELESS YOUNG PEOPLE: A STRATEGY OF ATTENTION
    Constance Ellwood

CHAPTER 3 53
    RELATIONALITY AND THE ART OF BECOMING
    Catherine Camden Pratt

CHAPTER 4 69
    DIFFERENCE AS ETHICAL ENCOUNTER
    Susanne Gannon

CHAPTER 5 89
    BECOMING BLOSSOM, BECOMING ODDBOD: CLOWNING AS TRANSFORMATIONAL PROCESS
    Constance Ellwood and Catherine Camden Pratt

CHAPTER 6 105

REFLECTIONS ON A DAY IN THE ART CLASS
Bronwyn Davies, Katerina Zabrodska, Susanne Gannon, Peter Bansel and Catherine Camden Pratt

CHAPTER 7 131

SECOND SKIN: THE ARCHITECTURE OF PEDAGOGICAL ENCOUNTERS
Bronwyn Davies, Catherine Camden Pratt, Constance Ellwood, Susanne Gannon, Katerina Zabrodska and Peter Bansel

BIBLIOGRAPHY 151

LIST OF AUTHORS 157

INDEX 159

ACKNOWLEDGMENTS

This project was supported by the Australian Research Council Discovery grant, *Enabling Place Pedagogies in Rural and Urban Australia*, awarded to M. Somerville, B. Davies, K. Power and S. Gannon in 2006–2008. The Sydney group made up of Davies and Gannon used the methodology of collective biography to explore the related concepts of pedagogy and place. This book grew out of the collective biography workshops, which were funded by the ARC grant, as was the later art workshop, and the writing retreat where most of the authors of the various chapters of this book worked together on each of the chapters. The ethnographic study in Chapter Three was funded by the College of Arts at the University of Western Sydney. The trip to observe and open up dialogue in Reggio Emilia inspired preschools in Italy and Sweden, which Bronwyn undertook in 2008, was funded by the ARC grant, by the Reggio Emilia Institute in Sweden, and by Uppsala University.

We would like to thank those various readers and audiences who have responded to earlier drafts. Hillevi Lenz Taguchi and her research group at Stockholm University gave invaluable feedback to an earlier draft of the book. Audiences who responded to lectures given by Bronwyn based on various parts of this work include: pedagogues and members of the International Centre at Reggio Children; members of the Stockholm Reggio Emilia Institute; people attending the conference on Gender Education and the Body at Lancaster University; and the audiences at papers given at Kalmar University, Uppsala University, and Melbourne University. We are indebted to those audiences for their feedback, their enthusiasm and their questions.

The authors of each of the chapters have contributed generous feedback on all of the chapters, and Peter Bansel gave insightful and generous feedback on the final draft. While most chapters are written by single authors, this book has been an exercise in Nancy's *Being Singular Plural*: engaged in a process of being *with,* of being "singulars singularly together" (2000: 33); "beginning from the 'with,' *as the proper essence of the one whose Being is nothing other than with-one-another*" (2000: 34).

INTRODUCTION
BRONWYN DAVIES

We began this book at a collective biography workshop that Susanne and I convened in a house at Bombo on the south coast of New South Wales. The five of us, Susanne and I, along with Constance, Catherine and Katerina, the authors of chapters in this book, spent a week together, looking out over the wild seascape, cooking meals for each other, talking and reading and telling stories, drawing on, and drawing out, our own memories, searching for ways to rethink the relations between pedagogy and place/space. We wanted to explore the relations between those pedagogical spaces and places that we remembered, and student–teacher subjectivities and relations.

In this book we think of place making as a relational form of art, and as an artful form of relationality. Place making focuses on relations with others, including non-human animate and inanimate others. Its artfulness lies both in what we usually think of as art, and also in the art of becoming—of being vulnerable and open to the unknown and to the other. Pedagogical relationality as art opens up the possibility of learning differently, of "creat[ing] meaning through entanglements and spatial re-alignments" (Springgay, 2008: 95), of becoming reflexive, creative makers of meaning, rather than mere recipients of over-coded, fixed knowledges.

Good teaching is often conceived as the successful imposition of a desirable order on an otherwise unbearable chaos—the chaos of multiple bodies, multiple ways of knowing, diverse trajectories, opposing wills, which must be brought into line and contained. But the relation between chaos and order is not best understood in binary terms. In this book we will explore, rather, a dynamic relation in which chaos and order co-exist. Order may generate a safe place in which creativity and innovation can be fostered, leading to the transformation of matter and life in unpredictable ways. Order may also work to preclude such excess, privileging the already known. From a Deleuzian perspective, safe spaces are a necessary base—an orderly plane—from which creative transformations can emerge. At the same time, the evolution of life emerges not from uniformity and sameness but from the "differentiation of life forms from each other...[and], above all, in their becoming-artistic, in their self-transformations, which exceed the bare requirements of existence" (Grosz, 2008a: 6).

Such an approach to education may seem to be out of reach, given the relations between schools, government and capitalism. Schools service capitalism insofar as they produce workers capable both of producing and purchasing material goods. But they may also produce life in excess of capitalism, capable of critiquing forms of power and domination (including capitalism itself). They are capable, we will argue, of generating new forms of life—forms not based on what is already known, but on the not-yet-known. It is in this sense that the making of pedagogical places and spaces is a form of art where "Art enables matter to become expressive, to not just satisfy but also to intensify—to resonate and become more than itself" (Grosz, 2008a: 4).

Sometimes schools do provide a place in which becoming-artistic is fostered, and in which both collective and individual evolution and transformation can occur (see for example Springgay, 2008). Or they can try, as many currently feel impelled to do, in response to government surveillance and funding mechanisms, to order existence to fit a prescribed set of outcomes that tie teachers and students into the already known.

The overweening desire on the part of government agencies for prescriptive controls, and for reining students and teachers in, is arguably intimately linked with the dangers, or what Deleuze and Guattari called the "schizophrenia" of capitalism. Schizophrenia is "both the 'limit' and the 'logic' of global capitalism" (Hickey-Moody and Malins, 2007: 4). In Deleuze's and Guattari's analysis "the capitalist machine does not run the risk of becoming mad, it is mad from one end to another...and this is the source of its rationality" (1987: 373). From this analytic perspective:

> [C]apitalism is able to harness the energy generated by deterritorialized and decoded flows of desire, turning it into flows of money and goods, flows of profit. It is in this sense that capitalism succeeds in performing a new level of social oppression and repression. Capitalism does not seek to prevent the desire flows of bodies, but instead seeks to ensure that those flows are always already functioning for capitalism. (Hickey-Moody and Malins, 2007: 15)

To this end capitalism territorializes teachers' work with end-driven rationalities that (pre)determine what is possible, what is desirable. Mindful of its own madness it creates an order that stifles the creativity it depends on for the metamorphoses and changes that are its life-blood. It is thus ironic, though predictable if we accept the metaphor of schizophrenia, that the success of capitalism requires those processes of becoming-artistic, those excesses, that the managerialism intrinsic to neoliberalism, or late capitalism, shuts down (Davies and Bansel, 2007a, 2007b).[i]

Deleuze's and Guattari's (1987) work is situated at this interface of capitalism's over-determined order, and the necessity for evolution, for life itself, to find ways to move beyond those controls. They seek out the "active positive lines of flight...[that] open up desire, desire's machines and the organization of a social field of desire...Opening up flows beneath social codes that seek to channel and block them" (Guattari in Deleuze, 1995: 19). It is this precise space that this book enters, between the over-coded striations of so much current schooling, and the lines of flight, that are necessary, in a Deleuzian perspective, for evolution, for life itself.

Capitalism is, by its nature, Deleuze and Guattari argue, constantly in flux, breaking things open to bring about new ideas. It depends on the state to be regulative in order to channel that creative energy toward the flow of capital. But in pedagogical spaces, neoliberal managerialism has taken externally driven regulation to such extremes that the new is at risk of being shut down—with only the already-known being recirculated inside its tightly regulated relations of power.

The neoliberal imagination, true to its capitalist origins, is consumed with the desire for end-products and for the technologies that will produce those end-products. That obsessional focus is antithetical to thought and to ethics, to debate, and to the necessary uncertainty that fuels new ideas (Rinaldi, 2006). The managerial mechanisms of neoliberalism have been developed and refined over the last three decades of neoliberal ascendancy such that they are apparently inescapable. "There is no alternative" is its constant refrain. Neoliberal technologies are secured at the systemic level by being tied to government funding, and at the individual level, to job tenure and the mechanisms for assessing professional performance.

Intrinsic to these mechanisms is an emphasis on individuality and competition. Individuals are made responsible for their own survival and set in competition against each other in their will to survive. Each individual's desire to survive, in competition with others, is used by governing agencies to require that each individual become the externally driven flexible subject, capable of producing whatever the agency (or capital) desires. In the guise of freedom—productivity and the consumption of products becomes what each person wants—the desire of governing agencies and of capital becomes the desire of each individual. For researchers and teachers this means they must be ready (flexible enough, desiring enough) to reshape their practices in response to whatever the latest directive is. They must even be flexible enough to lose their job without complaint if their response is not what is required of them by management.

As successive neoliberal governments shed their responsibility for welfare, individuals are taught to become risk aversive, since there will be no safety net if they make mistakes. Reduced security means that personal safety/survival becomes a dominant value, and if it can only be secured through unquestioning obedience, then desire flows toward finding out what the latest performance measures are and learning how to perform in terms of them. The newly individualized, vulnerable subject of neoliberalism must avoid risk, and seek out safety and predictability thus taking up as their own desire the perpetuation of the suffocating striations of government (Davies and Bansel, 2007a, 2007b).

Thinking outside the neoliberal framework has taken a great deal of courage. Early childhood education has taken a lead on this front (see for example Dahlberg, Moss and Pence, 1999; Lenz Taguchi, 2009; Moss and Petrie, 2002; Dahlberg and Moss, 2005; Rinaldi, 2006). At the time of writing many are reading the global economic crises as signaling the end of neoliberalism: "The great neo-liberal experiment of the past 30 years has failed" (Rudd, 2009: 23). It is timely, then, for this book to extend that work in the early childhood arena, of developing pedagogical thought against the grain of neoliberal imperatives, to the whole of schooling.

That approach is one of openness to relationality, to an ongoing process of becoming, in dialogue with others, both in and across communities. It seeks to open up a new kind of flexibility, not externally driven, but responsive, relational, artistic and life-giving—insofar as life is generated through a continual Deleuzian unfolding of thought and practice. The tasks of education within capitalism, we want to argue, are not to order and contain, but to give permission—to provide processes where research and teaching are contiguous, where the creative engagement with ideas enables the crossing of boundaries, the opening up of new questions, new ways of asking questions, and of answering them, in an ongoing, dynamic, relational framework. Such a framework would skill people up to engage with philosophy, the arts and sciences in ways that fertilize imagination and movement. It would protect students against their own possible madness within capitalism by enabling a relatively or sufficiently stable positioning within relational networks. It would generate new understandings of subjectivity, of the impact of discourses of capitalism and neoliberalism on subjectivity, and of relationality and responsibility to self and other. Such a framework would enable reflexive, analytic and ethical awareness, enabling the subject not to be simply caught within the flows of madness, but able to utilize them, to become-artistic within them, and also to critique them, and resist them, thus opening them up to transformation.

To this end Deleuze sought to prise us loose from a fixation on individual egos and to entice us into the ongoing practice of becoming—opening ourselves to difference in ourselves and in the other, the other being not just other human beings, but the physical objects, landscapes and other materialities and intensities with which and in which we take up our existence.

Spaces of learning

Throughout this book we will open up the possibility of a Deleuzian becoming in educational settings including preschools, primary and secondary schools, universities and communities. To do so we weave together three separate threads: the philosophy and practice of collective biography (Davies and Gannon, 2006); the Deleuzian spatial turn in poststructuralist theorizing; and the philosophy and practices of Reggio Emilia schooling, which has close connections to Deleuzian thought (Dahlberg and Moss, 2005; Lenz Taguchi, 2009). Although we began this work with a concept of place, Deleuze rapidly took us to the concept of space. Whereas place signifies a somewhere that already has an identity, space signals a place that is not fixed, and that is open to multiplicity. A Deleuzian vocabulary invites us to consider how we might think of ourselves, and perform ourselves, differently, how we might let go of some part of our individualism and open up the possibility of new ways of thinking about who we are in relation to others and in relation to place.

At the heart of the book are stories of pedagogical encounters, which we have generated in collective biography workshops, in ethnographic projects and in observations of Reggio Emilia inspired preschools. We examine the ways in which students and their teachers come into being in multiple ways in their encounters with each other, becoming-artistic, transforming themselves in relation to each other and to the spaces they create. These stories take place in Australia, in the Czech Republic and in

Sweden. They are sometimes in state-run, publicly funded schools or organizations, and sometimes in independent organizations.

The emphasis given to Reggio Emilia here may seem surprising given its location primarily in preschool settings, while our interest stretches from early childhood to adult education. The book that drew us to the Reggio Emilia philosophy was Ceppi's and Zini's (1998) *Children, Spaces, Relations. Metaproject for an environment for young children*. This book was written from an architectural perspective about creating spaces that are facilitative of learning. An architectural approach to learning is particularly interesting in a Deleuzian analysis. As Grosz points out, from a Deleuzian perspective:

> Art is first architectural...Architecture is the most elementary binding or containment of forces, the conditions under which qualities can live their own life through the constitution of territory...each [architectural] form of life, and each cultural form, undertakes its own modes of organization, its own connections of body and earth, its own management of the intractable problems that impose themselves on the living...Art captures an element, a fragment, of chaos in the frame and creates or extracts from it not an image or representation, but a sensation or rather a compound or multiplicity of sensations... (Grosz, 2008a: 16, 18)

That "multiplicity of sensations" that is generated in specific places of learning is deeply implicated in the processes of learning. Ceppi and Zini point out that neurobiology "has clearly demonstrated the co-protagonism of the senses in the construction and processing of knowledge and individual and group memory" (1998: n.p.). Indeed, according to Lehrer (2007: 20) neurobiologists have shown that the rational mind cannot actually function without the senses: "the feelings generated by the body are an essential element of rational thought...[so much so that those without emotion] are incapable of making rational decisions." Ceppi and Zini conceive of pedagogical places as multisensory, where pedagogy is designed to heighten the learners' sensory capacities, along with their capacity to respond to the others (both animate and inanimate) around them. They envisage a pedagogy that holds together the idea of the learner as both an idiosyncratic, unique individual and a member of an intensely interrelated community of learners.

Learners are, in Nancy's terms, both singular and plural; they are engaged in a process of being *with*, of being "singulars singularly together" (2000: 33). The "rich normality" of Ceppi's and Zini's imagined

INTRODUCTION

learning community assumes and invites diversity, openness to the other and to new ways of being oneself and being together. The future in such a community is genuinely open.

Ceppi's and Zini's architectural orientation envisages the material space of the school as integral to learning, not separate from students and their work but integral to it. The students' documentation of their unfolding thoughts and sensations, for example, is displayed on the walls of the school to form a second "psychic skin." That "skin" is alive, and energy giving and it is high in aesthetic and pedagogical value. The school becomes:

> An environment that documents not only the results but also the processes of learning and knowledge-building, that narrates the didactic paths and states the values of reference. The environment generates a sort of psychic skin, an energy giving second skin made of writings, images, materials, objects, and colors, which reveals the presence of the children even in their absence. (Ceppi and Zini, 1998: n.p.)

This movement, the emergence of the second skin, undoes the binary that separates individual subjects from others—both animate and inanimate. The places that we call classrooms and schools are reconceptualized as spaces made up of multiple, emergent, related subjects. The art work that forms the second psychic skin, is not just an extension of already established individualized subjects, or a representation of those subjects or of others external to them, but is an other in relation, and generative of new relations and becomings.

In elaborating the spatial turn in the Reggio Emilia context, Ceppi and Zini write about Reggio Emilia inspired preschools as providing spaces that are "more open to the indeterminableness of experience [where the] environment is conceived not as a monologic space structured according to a formal framework and a functional order, but a place where multiple dimensions coexist—even opposing ones" (1998: n.p.). They define space as shaped by the relationships within it. Architecturally speaking, they are interested in places that are "constructed not by selecting and simplifying the elements, but through a fusion of distinct poles (inside and outside, formality and flexibility, material and immaterial)" (Ceppi and Zini, 1998: n.p.). The focus on students and teachers in this re-thinking of place and space is no longer on individualized subjects, but on beings emerging in relation, beings emergent in their interactions with others (including both human and non-human, animate and inanimate others), and with the surrounding multi-logic space of which those other beings are part (Macy, 1991). It is the focus on relationality in this re-thinking that shifted this book from its beginning in pedagogy and place to its emergence as *Pedagogical Encounters*. Those encounters are with human others, and with all those animate and inanimate others who populate and create the relational spaces we are part of.

Deleuze and Guattari, emphasize that space is far more than a passive backdrop to human action. Space as they conceive it is active in shaping what is possible. It is, in Roy's words:

> [T]he topographic characteristics of space, often made invisible and pushed into the background by existing assumptions and force of habit, determine the possibilities and limits of what may occur within it. The term 'space' here is not metaphorical…but geo-ontological. (Roy, 2005: 29)

Collective biography

The collective biography stories in this book come primarily from the workshop that Susanne and I ran on pedagogy and place in a house by the sea at Bombo, a small town on the New South Wales south coast. Susanne and I also ran a workshop with teacher education students on pedagogy and place, and later an art workshop, where we engaged in a pedagogical experiment, becoming art students and working with the stories we had generated in the collective biography workshop.

Collective biography is a research strategy peculiarly suited to the complex questions we are raising here, working at the level of bodily knowledge and of affect, and moving beyond individualized versions of the subject, toward subjects-in-relation, subjects-in-process (Davies and Gannon, 2006). It is particularly apt for place-based work, as relationships to place are constituted in stories (Somerville, 2008). In this complex task of re-membering ourselves and others in these spatial-relational terms in pedagogical spaces, and inspired by Ceppi and Zini (1998), we asked ourselves:

- What spaces can we remember that we have taught or learnt in, that we might think of as having a "second skin"?
- What spaces can we remember that were formed by the relations within them?
- What strategies of listening and of attention can we remember, focusing on the management of contradictions and conflicts?

INTRODUCTION

- What transformative spaces can we remember where something different, or transformative became possible?

The practice of collective biography involves researchers as participants, over several consecutive days, meeting and talking about their chosen topic, telling their own remembered stories relevant to that topic, and writing them down. The relationship between the participants and the written texts, and memories evoked in the workshop space, is developed through a particular kind of close attention to each other's stories. Through listening and questioning each other on the remembered, embodied, affective detail, each story becomes imaginable with/in the minds/bodies of everyone. After telling stories, and listening to stories, and talking together about those stories, they are written, avoiding clichés and explanations. Each story is then read out loud to the group, registering the images now in the written form, and heard again in the modality of voice, through the vibrations in the bodies of speakers and listeners.

In the writing and reading, in the discussion about, and questioning of the read text, and in the rewriting, each storyteller works to express the very this-ness, or haecceity, of the remembered moment. Haecciety or this-ness, as Halsey analyses it, is integral to what Deleuze calls smooth space—the space that escapes the over-coded striations of territorialized space. Smooth space enables an immersion in the present moment, in time and in place, that often eludes us in the press of normative expectations, of habitual thoughts and practices, and of submission to the dominant, often clichéd codes that make up the existing order.

In our book, *Doing Collective Biography* (2006), Susanne and I coined the term mo(ve)ment in order to evoke the doubled action involved in our collective story-telling and writing, of dwelling in and on particular moments of being, and of movement toward, or openness to, new possibilities both of seeing and of being. In telling, listening, questioning, writing, reading and rewriting our stories, a shift takes place. The memories are no longer told and heard as just autobiographical (that is, an assemblage of already known stories that mark one individualized person off from the next), but as opening up for, and in, each other, knowledges of being that previously belonged only to the other, as that other's marks of identity. In working collectively with memories, we live intimately within our own bodies, and our bodies take on the intimate knowledge of each other's being. Each subject's specificity in its very particularity, in its sensory detail, becomes, through this process, the collectively imagined detail through which we know ourselves as human, even as more human—as humans-in-relation.

Participation in collective biography extends the capacity for listening, and develops a new understanding and practice of relationality not unlike that which Rinaldi describes as the kind of listening she envisages in pedagogical spaces. Such listening begins with:

> ...the courage to abandon yourself to the conviction that our being is just a small part of a broader knowledge; listening is a metaphor for listening to others, sensitivity to listen and be listened to, with all your senses...Behind each act of listening there is desire, emotion, and openness to differences, to different values and points of view...Learning how to listen is a difficult undertaking; you have to open yourself to others...Competent listening creates a deep opening and predisposition toward change. (Rinaldi, 2006: 114)

Within collective biography workshops, through developing the skills of listening and attending to the minute bodily detail of moments of being, it becomes possible for each story to become a collective story, its purpose no longer to signal the substance of any particular individual, but to open the participants to new insights into the processes of being and becoming in the world—new ways of being subjects (Davies et al., 2006):

> The poststructural subject-in-process in our collective biography writing is one who plays between a close and detailed observation of what she finds when she examines her memories, (un)hampered by the moorings of liberal humanist signifying practices, *and* one who recognizes the constitutive force of that same moment of speaking/writing such a description. In this sense the poststructural subject might be said to exist at the site of an almost intolerable contradiction, a contradiction that is necessary to comprehend subjectification. Butler says of this necessary ambivalence: "...the subject is itself a site of this ambivalence in which the subject emerges both as the *effect* of a prior power and as the *condition of possibility* for a radically conditioned form of agency. A theory of the subject should take into account the full ambivalence of the conditions of its operation" (Butler, 1997: 14-15). In that ambivalence our subject-in-process finds herself quite powerful, not so caught in definitions of herself as she might have been. She finds herself in mo(ve)ments, and as she *scrapes* her way through poststructural writing, *catches* herself in the act of being subjected, and, sometimes, she *drags* her individualized subjecthood behind her. She is above all, in process, vulnerable to inscriptions that may be opaque to her and yet developing the

INTRODUCTION

powers to make the discourses and their inscriptive powers both visible and revisable. (Davies et al., 2006: 181)

The stories told and written in collective biography workshops do not claim to be representations of the real, or to tell a final truth of "what happened" though they do not intentionally deviate from what is remembered. Rather they are experienced as deeply inscribed on the bodies of the storytellers and listeners through their embodied senses. Collective biography story-telling takes place in a specific time and place, with particular others who, in their specificity and difference, invoke new becomings, as their memories call forth one's own. The stories are unpredictable, surprising and always mediated by others—the others in the workshop and the others in the stories, who are also there-in-the-telling.

The practices of collective biography, like Reggio Emilia preschools, thus build a communal space through "the willingness to listen and be open to others...[and through] respect for differences, however they may be expressed...[It is a] sense of empathy, a closeness that creates bonds, that enables each group member to recognize the other and to recognize him/herself in the other" (Ceppi and Zini, 1998: n.p.).

When the other is different, and has made different, initially unimaginable choices, the processes of collective biography enable each participant to know—through attending to affect, to emotion, to voice, to images, to the specificity of the other—the rich and surprising multiplicity of their own and others' being. It opens up a means of being *with*, of being "singulars singularly together" (Nancy, 2000: 33); it is a process that begins "from the 'with'" (Nancy, 2000: 34), and while recovering the singular specificity of the one, it understands the one to be *"nothing other than with-one-another"* (Nancy, 2000: 34).

Affect is as important as language in creating that relational space. Affect signals openness to intensity, to seeing up close, to seeing in other ways to the habitual, striated or over-coded ways of seeing. In Hickey-Moody's and Malins' words:

> Affect is that which is felt before it is thought; it has a visceral impact on the body before it is given subjective or emotive meaning. Thinking through affect brings the sensory capacity of the body to the fore. When we encounter an image of a bomb victim, smell milk that has soured, or hear music that is out of key, our bodies tense before we can articulate an aversion...Affect is, therefore, very different from emotion: it is an a-subjective bodily response

to an encounter. Emotion comes later, as a classifying or stratifying of affect...As a concept, 'affect' enables us to think about how certain assemblages, languages or social institutions impact on bodies in ways that are not conscious. (Hickey-Moody and Malins, 2007: 8)

Beginning, then, with our collective biography stories, we explore throughout this book an emergent pedagogy that focuses in particular on relationality and on univocity—the embeddedness of each human being in relations with others and with the physical and psychic environment in which teachers and students find themselves. The pedagogical environment we seek in our interactions with each other and that we imagine for classrooms, is, like the spaces Ceppi and Zini describe in the Reggio Emilia context:

> A space that is responsive and transformable that enables different ways of inhabitance and use during the course of the day and with the passing of time. The space should also be personalizable, soft, open to receiving imprints. Designing a school is like writing a film treatment, while the screenplay is written by those who inhabit the school and construct its identity day by day. The space, then, like a living organism, must be able to change and evolve in line with the cultural project of those who inhabit it, while maintaining the genetic characteristics of the design project. (Ceppi and Zini, 1998: n.p.)

We seek to unfold something here, in this book, through our stories woven together with concepts from Reggio Emilia pedagogy and from Deleuzian and other scholars, that is both continuous with the already-known, and yet unfolding itself into the not-yet-known. In places of learning, we will suggest, all the matter that is available in the pedagogical assemblage, can be understood as emergent and endlessly differentiating itself on the same plane, with each potentially affecting and being affected by every other. We seek in our stories to find those moments that might be called Deleuzian lines of flight, "Opening up flows beneath social codes that seek to channel and block them" (Deleuze, 1995: 19).

The emergent pedagogy we are working on here begins with the moments of being that are encompassed in each of our stories. These are stories that dwell on and in the particularity of pedagogical encounters, encounters that are sometimes deeply moving, and sometimes distressing; they are stories that are both historically specific and yet open

INTRODUCTION

out into future, emergent possibilities that go beyond the limitations of current pedagogical thought.

This book is an experiment in writing, and it is a deeply felt response to the ways in which current pedagogies are constrained by neoliberal technologies and practices. Collectively we have sought new ways of thinking of pedagogy, and of finding ways to open up the future rather than close it down. It involves rethinking what it means to be a human subject, how that subject comes to know differently, and what it means to be subjects in relation, responsive to each other, emergent in our encounters with each other.

Overview of chapters

In Chapter One, *Difference and differenciation*, I explore the Deleuzian concepts of difference and differenciation. Deleuzian concepts are intended to unsettle old ways of thinking, inviting us to engage in life as a series of encounters that unfold out into the not-yet-known. The category of difference as categorical difference, in which entities are understood as multiple, diverse and separate, gives way here to the category of differenciation. Deleuze gives primacy to differenciation over difference, which he defines as a continuous process of becoming different. The stories in this chapter each hold a moment of encounter. Some of these stories are from collective biography workshops and some are from my own memories and ethnographic observations. All happen to be set in early childhood settings. I use these encounters to unsettle habitual modes of thought—to unsettle the territorializations and striations that make up what we take for granted as "schools" and "classrooms." This chapter concludes with the discussion of a new ethics, envisaging an ethical-aesthetic life not trapped in the already known.

Chapter Two, *Listening to homeless young people: a strategy of attention*, by Constance, moves into the space of Oasis, a school for homeless youth. The students' lives at this school have been marked by failures—those of their families, their schools and themselves. The teacher/researcher develops the concept and practice of a *strategy of attention*. This is a strategy taken up by teachers in this school that make learning possible for students that the state system cannot manage. This chapter explores the dynamics of "the willingness to listen and be open to others which is fundamental to any educational context" (Ceppi and Zini, 1998: n.p.). It shows how this strategy of attention is fundamental to productive relationships between teachers and students, particularly when those students' ways of being in the world are not what teachers normally recognize as acceptable or even comprehensible. The chapter draws on the Reggio Emilia metaphor of one hundred languages (Rinaldi, 2006) to discuss the multiple ways the students in this classroom have for communicating and for creating, with their teachers, a sense of community. The stories of the homeless youth at Oasis are contrasted with stories from an ethnographic study by Youdell, where similar students are regarded as impossible strangers, who teachers find themselves unable to recognize or respect.

In Chapter Three, *Relationality and the art of becoming*, Catherine works with a story of art making and becoming in a kindergarten classroom. It tells of a traumatised child caught up in her world of artistic expression and a teacher caught in the binds of striated space struggling to find, and finding, other possibilities for the children and their teacher which are opened up by one child's line of flight. The teacher, along with the other children, both hold the molar order of the classroom in place and, at the same time, deterritorialize the focus on pre-set curricula and pre-specified products, opening up the possibility of moving into the not-yet-known. The teacher's response to the child takes her on her own line of flight, and she opens up that possibility to the other children in her classroom. This chapter explores the place of art making in becoming and the ways in which art making opens up lines of flight which take the artist into the world of chaos and return her as a transformed subject. It also explores respect for differences, however they may be expressed, where each child has room to engage in private, even seemingly strange, work, and room to join in, to be safely the same within the co-ordinates of the classroom's orderly and ordering practices.

Chapter Four, *Difference as ethical encounter*, by Susanne, extends the concept of difference, drawing new theorists into the framing of this work—in particular Ahmed, Bell and Levinas. Focusing on ethnic and racial differences she explores the ways in which categorical differences become embedded (in bodies, in language, in cultures, in nations) and have effects. The stories in this chapter involve foreign exchange students in the far north east of Australia and indigenous students in the far north west. For the students in both of these stories their first language is different from the dominant language used in the classroom. This chapter theorizes the ethics of encounter in the context of such classrooms, and extends the concept of pedagogical encounter by drawing on the speech

INTRODUCTION

given by the Prime Minister of Australia, in which he apologized to the stolen generation. The chapter draws on this speech to extend the analysis of pedagogy through the possibility of collective movement brought about in, and in response to, this speech.

Chapter Five, *Becoming Blossom, becoming Oddbod: Clowning as transformational process,* by Constance and Catherine, takes us into another landscape altogether. Set in the decaying gardens of a colonial home that became a mental asylum, the Drama Action Centre emerged in our collective biography stories-so-far as a significant place for two members of our group who had been students there in the 1990s. The stories of the two clowns, Oddbod and Blossom, bring us into the process of differenciation and becoming from the point of view of the students, allowing us to see just how the strategy of attention of teacher, and of audience, work to make possible the emergent possibility of self that is other than who one was before. The shedding of individualism and the openness to movement toward a new way of thinking and being is not easily accomplished—it is a painful and peculiar process in which the static striations of identity are peeled open. Working with the concept of affect, and focusing on the embodied presence of the learner and her co-extension with objects and subjects with whom she interacts, the approach that is unfolded here dwells on the capacity for the learner and the teacher to work toward that which is real and true: becoming clown involves a production of the real (Deleuze and Parnet, 1987: 49); it involves "playing the truth game" and recognizing that "[T]he less defensive one is, the less one tries to play a character, and the more one allows oneself to be surprised by one's own weaknesses, the more forcefully one's clown will appear" (LeCoq et al., 2001: 145 translation modified). Allowing oneself to be vulnerable emerges us a crucial step in opening up the space to movement—an idea that also emerges in the subsequent chapter.

In Chapter Six, *Reflections on a day in the art class,* Peter, Catherine, Susanne, Katerina and I collectively give ourselves over to being students together in an art workshop. We enter the space that enables us to put our linear stories and analytic strategies to one side and to give ourselves over to the emergent process of art making. We are each vulnerable and afraid in the face of our own lack of skill, and to the affective space we have given ourselves over to. Yet we are at the same time held safe by our young teachers who take on the task of running our workshop, enabling us to explore the art of becoming as students in an art classroom. Our teachers, Jade and Alicia demonstrate a strategy of attention, a capacity to listen, to be present, to step in, when we find ourselves confronted by the limitations of our rational plans and our limited skills. Here, Deleuze's observation that differenciation is first and foremost individual is made evident in the deeply personal struggle that each engages in. Barely aware of each other, at times, we are, at the same time, held safe in the space of the art classroom, made up of rough wooden tables, used tubes of paint, a richness of objects to work with, and the quiet presence of the teachers and the other students—each engaged in their own works of art, each *with-the-other* in creating the space that makes the singular work possible.

Chapter Seven, *Second skin: the architecture of pedagogical encounters*, written by Catherine, Constance, Susanne, Katerina and Bronwyn, focuses on Ceppi's and Zini's concept of psychic, second skin. In this final chapter we turn our attention to the environments in which learning has or has not happened in various pedagogical contexts in university settings. We find a particular, peculiar power in the physical spaces that envelop us in these contexts—sometimes a power that appears to make thought impossible, to shut down the possibility of anything new; and sometimes a power that lifts us up and lends us an intensity and joy that is energizing and creative. The metaphor of second skin is potent in lending a rich presence to the concept of univocity—or co-extension with the subjects and objects around us. It enables us to understand vividly that the individual subject is not immune to context, but also, that context itself is not immune to us. Context is understood here as a set of forces, but not as a determining force. It is an actor in the assemblage that makes up any pedagogical encounter, now intruding and taking over, now receding in its power and significance.

Notes

[i] There have been many descriptions of neoliberalism. In the face of the global economic crisis, Australian Prime Minister Kevin Rudd refers to it as "that particular brand of free-market fundamentalism, extreme capitalism and excessive greed which became [in the last 30 years] the economic orthodoxy of our time" (Rudd, 2009: 20. See also Davies, Gottsche and Bansel, 2006).

1
DIFFERENCE AND DIFFERENCIATION
Bronwyn Davies

In the Introduction I sketched out the ways in which neoliberal managerialism has generated pedagogies that are closed and end-product driven and that heighten individualism and competition *against* the other. I suggested an alternative form of pedagogy that was relational and involved an ongoing art of becoming. I did not set these in binary opposition to each other but as able to exist in the same place, working together in unexpected ways. The most important conceptual shift that Deleuze offers us for re-thinking the ways in which we might open up the territorialized and over-coded striations of schooling is the move from difference to differenciation.

Philosophy has, following Aristotle, conceptualized difference as categorical difference, in which the other is discrete and distinct from the self, with the difference lying in the other (black to my white, male to my female, straight to my queer). Deleuze offers another approach to difference in which difference comes about through a continuous process of becoming different, of differenciation. Massey (2005: 21) describes these two approaches as:

1. "discrete difference/multiplicity (which refers to extended magnitudes and distinct entities, the realm of diversity)," and

2. "continuous difference/multiplicity (which refers to intensities, and to evolution rather than succession)."

In the first approach difference is being "divided up, a dimension of separation" while in the second, Deleuzian approach, difference is "a continuum, a multiplicity of fusion." Deleuze wishes "to instate the significance, indeed the philosophical primacy, of the second (continuous) form of difference over the first (the discrete) form. What is at issue is an insistence on the genuine openness of history, of the future" (Massey, 2005: 21). As Williams (2003: 60) points out, for Deleuze "real difference is a matter of how things become different, how they evolve and continue to evolve beyond the boundaries of the sets they have been distributed into."

In what follows I will draw on a number of stories to flesh out this distinction between difference and differenciation, to bring it to life in pedagogical space. The first story here was written from my own memory while struggling with this new understanding of difference:

The small boy, in the week before first going to school, was playing joyfully with another child, who was going to go to the same school as he was to go to. His mother had invited her to play, having just met her parents who were new to the town—and to the country. The mother was happy watching them jumping up and down on the bed, and repeatedly falling down and laughing. It was the happiest she had seen him for a very long time. Then at school he did not play with her and he did not want her to visit any more.

Had he discovered, the mother wondered, that she was a girl and that boys did not play with girls? Or had he discovered she was black, and that white children did not play with black children?

The only explanation he could give his mother as to why he did not play with her was that she sniffed. This did not make sense to the mother, since he too was a child who sniffed, having not yet fully mastered the use of hankies.

If we approach the story in terms of the first conception of difference, it is a categorical difference that had been generated in the new setting of the school that inexorably separated the children from each other. The mother imagines it is the categories of gender or race that have divided them. The boy tells her it is the category of people who sniff. But he is in that same category so the mother cannot understand his explanation and their communication breaks down.

In contrast, if we approach the story through the Deleuzian conception of difference, in terms of intensities and evolution, then we see a joyful intensity in the first setting, with the boy becoming different in his intense engagement with the girl. *It was the happiest she had seen him for a very long time.* The space of the home makes possible this particular way of being and becoming, turning the bed into a trampoline, letting go, forgetting himself, and becoming someone new. But the space of the school works differently. What was possible at home is not possible here. The intensities and modes of becoming that are possible in this space do not make that same set of intensities possible. Before they went to school the child he played with was not separate; she was not the other;

DIFFERENCE AND DIFFERENCIATION

rather, she opened up intensities in him that invited him to become different from himself. The two children flowed together, in Deleuzian terms, in a third stream that they created together (Deleuze, 1990: 136). Being a person in this way of thinking is not to belong to a category, but more in the nature of an event, or a series of events.

This reconceptualizing of difference has strong implications for pedagogy. Williams describes how Deleuze highlights the way in which the primacy of the first kind of difference:

> ...has become imbedded in thinking and common sense—for example, in the way learning involves exercises of attribution in the early stages of development and, indeed, much later, in the form of tests (Where does this thing belong? In which of these boxes would you put this thing? What is the difference between this set of things and that one?...Tick one box.). (Williams, 2003: 59-60)

In a Deleuzian pedagogy, in contrast, all subjects and objects are open to becoming different from themselves. My second story comes from a recent visit to a Reggio Emilia inspired preschool in Stockholm:

There were some chairs in the room we met in that had become dogs. I was particularly intrigued by a chair that had become a poodle. As I walked toward it, and gazed at it, it was clearly a chair. The children had stuck popcorn all over the chair, and the head of the dog had grown out of what had once been the back of the chair. It was when I realized I could no longer sit on the chair, that I understood it had lost its chairness and taken on enchanting intensities of tight white curls and a prancing saucy pointy faced poodleness. But more, I discovered, in a second transformation, a second event, the plastic bags of popcorn that made the ears had been opened by little fingers intent on transforming the handsome poodle into a feast of popcorn. The tight white popcorn curls of its body were safe as they tasted bad from the lacquer painted over them.

This fluidity of categories would have delighted Deleuze. The chair differenciates itself into intensities of poodleness and then into a feast, holding all the while some sense of chairness and poodleness and feast. Differenciation is the term used to capture this Deleuzian sense of difference.

Roffe describes the Deleuzian space of differenciation or becoming as first, "a moment of de-individualization, an escape to some degree from the limits of the individual. Secondly there must be the constitution of new ways of being in the world, new ways of thinking and feeling, new ways of being a subject" (Roffe, 2007: 43). This conception of differenciation does not seek to fix subjects or objects in place, or tie them to static, individualistic, or binary identities, but opens up a space where creative energies are mobilized through ongoing relations within the spaces that are generated. Within the space of becoming, new ways of being and thinking are generated. This movement is not based on a rejection of the already-known, but on an assertion, rooted in philosophy, science and art, that life generates and is generated through movement and invention; it both draws on the already known, and it generates something new. The poodle did not reject the chair, but mobilized unexpected qualities in the chair to find the line of flight that made becoming-poodle possible.

A further major conceptual innovation in Deleuze's thinking concerns the nature of space and lines of force. How is it that one space opens up particular intensities and becomings and another does not? Deleuzian philosophy is intended to unsettle old ways of thinking about space, inviting us to engage in our lives as a series of encounters that open us up to the possibility of becoming members of "new kinds of society and new people" (Patton, 2007: ix). But that is not a categorical shift, moving from one kind of person to another. Not being fixed in their newness they cannot necessarily bring the new intensities with them (the joy of jumping together on the bed, for example), except in memory. Each event, each becoming, is necessarily new, while also building on the old. Life is emergent in Deleuzian philosophy, it continually evolves through the flows and intensities of each new encounter. One may remain within a habitual repeated series, or take off from the already-known in new lines of flight. Deleuze generates the concept of smooth space as the space in which such lines of flight take place, in which places locked into the striations of habituated repeated series, might be set loose—de-territorialized.

Territorial or "molar lines," in contrast to lines of flight, "organize by drawing strict boundaries, creating binary oppositions and dividing space into rigid segments with a hierarchical structure" (Woodward, 2007: 69). Molar lines create what Deleuze calls striated space.

> Striated spaces are those which are rigidly structured and organized, and which produce particular, limited movements and relations between bodies…Smooth spaces, by contrast, are those in which movement is less

DIFFERENCE AND DIFFERENCIATION

regulated or controlled, and where bodies can interact—and transform themselves—in endlessly different ways. (Hickey-Moody and Malins, 2007: 11).

What is so surprising about Deleuze, is that he brings together, again and again, the apparently irreconcilable, in provocative and productive ways. He asks us to think of these opposing lines, lines of flight and molar lines, and the smooth and striated spaces they create, not as alternatives, but as existing together in the same space. The molar lines of force create rigid striations, and at the same time offer places for experience and experimentation, in which new movements become possible, where old territories can be rethought, re-territorialized, where new connections can occur; where experi-mentation can open up a new line of flight. But even then, even in the moment of flight, it is necessary to have a "small plot of land," a place where the molar order keeps us safe (Deleuze and Guattari, 1987: 161).

The source of the third story that I will tell here, is multiple. It is about my own memory of playing at the sandbox in preschool, but it holds within it memories of watching my own children at play, as well as the children in my preschool studies (Davies 1989/2003; Davies and Kasama, 2004). It is a moment of becoming in a kindergarten classroom, where the molar striated order is open to the children's experimentation and difference.

Two children sit at the new sandbox. The sand is dry and white with fine grains, some of which sparkle and stick to their skin. They cup the dry sand in their hands and let it trickle through their fingers. They are waiting for instructions. The early morning light streams through the window and casts rectangular bars of shadow across the box. The sun warms the cold sand and their skin. The teacher places a big jug of water in each sandbox. The children look uncertain and glance around the classroom at what the others are doing. They scoop out a ditch and pour the water in. It escapes immediately. They try again and it escapes again. They scoop up the wet sand and squeeze it and plop handfuls of wet sand on top of each others' hands, racing each other to see who can do it fastest. They laugh. They work fast. They pat the castle that begins to emerge. It grows huge and solid and they pat it flat and hard, their hands flat and hard against the surface. First one, then the other, carefully scratches a small hole in the side, watching each other, responding to each other, digging deeper with small fingers, overcoming hesitation, seeing how deep the tunnel can go. The space under their fingernails is filled with wet sand. Suddenly the castle fractures and one side sheers off in a straight line. They laugh with delight and one begins a road up the newly revealed face of the mountain. A window is hollowed out to reveal a house under the hill.

The children are, in Deleuze's terms, differenciating themselves as they experience and experiment with the intensities of the sand and the water and their partner in play. The intensities of the children's play emerge in the folds of the relationship with each other and with the sand, the water and the sun. They are immersed in the folds that the space affords them, unfolding into the sand and water and sunlight, and enfolded into it.

> For Deleuze, following Leibniz, the relationship between bodies and spaces is one of folding. The world around us folds into our bodies; shaping not only our movements, postures, emotions and subjectivity, but also the very matter of which we are composed. We are folded by our genes, the food we consume and the air we breathe; by sound, texture, light and taste; by our relationship with others, and our interaction with the spaces around us. At the same time, bodies continually fold out into the world: shaping—and transforming—the spaces and places around them. (Malins, 2007: 157-8)

The play with the sand and the water is all absorbing, and joyful. The sand, like cloth, like their bodies, can be folded in many ways and brings forth unexpected intensities and new capacities. The pleasure is in the experience, the experimentation without a plan. It is not instrumental, or product-driven, but engaged, energized, and life-generating.

At the same time, their sense of safety is produced through the known and predictable striations of their classroom. Their time at the sand pit will be measured by the teacher. Their relations with each other are ordered by classroom rules of good behavior: they will sit at the sandbox as long as it is their turn; they will play co-operatively; they will give up the sandbox to others when they are told to do so; they will wash off the sand from their hands; only two will be at the box at any one time. In this sense the children simultaneously inhabit smooth and striated space, a space that is both open to the new, and a space that is tightly controlled. While striated spaces might limit the possibilities of change, they are also necessary for the production of familiar, safe places:

> Stratifications are comforting: they enable the chaos of the world to be reduced to discrete categories of meaning and structure. They are also

important, for they enable us to interact with the social world; to form relations with others and to have a political 'voice'. Yet it is essential that stratifications also be understood as limiting: they reduce the range of connections a body can make with the world around it; diminishing its potential for difference and becoming-other. (Malins, 2007: 153)

Striated space imposes binary thought, it cuts and divides objects into categories, and divides people from each other and from the spaces they inhabit. Such divisions can become dangerous in their power to control and restrict possibilities. In striated space the binaries become naturalized—the world is divided that way because it is that way—and they can create apparently insurmountable impediments to change. In smooth space those concepts may be invoked, but they may also dissolve. The boundary between self and sand, self and mountain, self and other may cease to have any useful meaning. Castles can become mountains, lines of fault can open new paths; the direction is not set. One is no longer limited by a preconceived idea of self, but immersed in a moment of becoming—folding, unfolding, being enfolded, enfolding earth, light, air, and other beings.

In discussing the fourth story that I will tell here, drawn from the collective biography workshop that Sue and I ran with teacher education students on the topic of pedagogy and place, I add the concept of haecceity. Haecceity or this-ness is integral to what Deleuze calls deterritorialized smooth space—the space that escapes over-coded striations. Smooth space enables an immersion in the present moment, in time and in space, that often eludes us in the press of normative expectations, of habitually repeated thoughts and practices. The boy in this story becomes immersed in an exploration of movement and co-extension, folding and unfolding himself into the smooth space around him. He is immersed in the haecceity of the moment, and so engaged in a process of becoming different, newly aware of himself and his body in relation to the space around him.

The red station wagon was parked in the front yard, boot open. Mum, unpacking the weekly shopping, presented me with the responsibility for a five kilo bag of brushed potatoes.

Watching the shopping bags accumulate beside the car, I swayed the bag to and fro. The sack seemed to have its own momentum, the arc of the swing becoming wider and wider, until the potatoes reached eye-level, suspended, before gravity thrust them in the reverse trajectory.

Through trial as much as bravado, I attempted a full 360 degrees. The potatoes swung the arm, the arm swung the potatoes. Each revolution faster, stronger. Inevitably, the centrifuge of an upward swing wrenched open the base of the bag.

Potatoes released into the air.

Silence.

And then brushed potatoes rained upon the ground. One landing on the blue-brick stairs, another beside the perennials. A potato rolling down the concrete path to the front gate. One under the lean of the letterbox. Finally, a thud on the station wagon roof. And two glaring eyes.

This story captures the precise haecceity or this-ness of the moment of co-extension with the weight of the bag of potatoes, and with the garden, the car, the falling potatoes, and his mother's eyes. In his exploration, his experimentation with the weight and velocity of the bag, the boy enters a vivid, smooth space.

> A haecceity is a moment of pure speed and intensity (an individuation)—like when a swimming body becomes-wave and is momentarily suspended in nothing but an intensity of forces and rhythms. Or like when body becomes-horizon such that it feels only the interplay between curves and surfaces and knows nothing of here and there, observer and observed. (Halsey, 2007:146)

The moment of potatoes and boy almost in flight, almost together in that flight, and the car and the mother and the muscles and gravity of movement are the very this-ness of haecceity, where haecceity is not "simply...a décor or a backdrop that situates subjects," rather it is the "entire assemblage in its individuated aggregate that is a haecceity" (Deleuze and Guattari, 1987: 262).

What also becomes evident in this story of the boy and the potatoes is that haecceity and smooth space can be dangerous. They are exploratory, not already territorialized with what is known, not contained within predictable striations. The mother's glaring eyes may herald disaster for the small boy. Lines of flight are not always or only productive of goodness, or desirable outcomes: they necessarily also hold the possibility of danger and fear.

In the fifth story, taken from my work on preschool children and gender, the danger and fear in response to the line of flight is stark. The child in the story, George, engages in a line of flight; he stops engaging in the habitual repetitions that mark him out as belonging in the category boy, thus moving outside his assigned gender category, outside the

DIFFERENCE AND DIFFERENCIATION

gendered striations in which boy means not-feminine, and girl means not-masculine. George momentarily becomes not-recognizable within the known categories, and this signals danger to another boy:

George, in floating yellow skirt and cape, runs down the slope shouting "I am the power." He comes over to talk to me. Another boy comes over to where he is standing, and punches him. George takes off the skirt, rolls it up, puts it under his arm, and punches the boy back.

The space of the preschool makes available the yellow skirt and cape. They are part of a kit that the teachers have used to engage all the children in imagining becoming caterpillars and turning into yellow butterflies. The concept of the cape, and flying, comes from super heroes, and also, for George, from a story I had read him called *Rita the Rescuer*. George doubles his power wearing two butterfly capes, one as a skirt and one as a cape and announces the power he feels as he runs down the slope with his skirt and cape flying. But another boy is provoked, seeing George's line of flight as wrong, as outside the molar lines of force, the striations that make up the gender order, that make his own masculinity make sense. The male-female binary works in such a way that the habituated, repeated practices through which each category is generated become not just the way the world is, but the way it should be. A predictable moral order is made possible through the categories.

With his punch, the boy who guards the molar/moral order re-establishes the binary gender order. He engages in category-maintenance work (letting George know he is getting his masculinity wrong), and abjection (expelling any desire to perform himself as feminine by hitting a boy who does so). He violently defends the division of the world into boys-who-are-not-feminine and girls-who-are-not-masculine. Through his violent confrontation he maintains the striated order that for him makes the world safe and predictable. Before he fights back, George divests himself of the feminine signifier, though not abjecting it, not dropping it on the ground (Davies, 2006). He holds onto it under his arm and fights with his trousers visible. His line of flight is dangerous, and he accepts the need to become the same as the other boy, to take up the category of boy through making his trousers visible and punching back.

The lines of flight in these stories are moments of both pleasure and danger. They are, in their very haecceity, intensely pleasurable moments of being and becoming, and they are always at risk of being blocked by molar striations that both self and others might impose. Those striations make the world predictable and safe for the boy who punches George, and for George they may make his life precarious.

In this reading, George's story is one about the mechanisms through which categorical difference is maintained. It is also possible to read this story in terms of differenciation and becoming-artistic. Grosz points out that art is both about creating territories and deterritorialization. If the gender categories define the territory of the preschool, its striations, then George's flight down the slope is an act of deterritorialization, which involves:

> ...cutting through territories, breaking up systems of enclosure and performance, traversing territory in order to retouch chaos, enabling something mad, asystematic, something of the chaotic outside to reassert and restore itself in and through the body, through works and events that impact the body. (Grosz, 2008a: 18)

George's flight can be read as a breaking open of the known order, a creative event in which he generates another possible order. He engages in an artistic becoming—in which his body and his voice interact with the yellow butterfly capes and the slope of the hill, to create a different territory, one not divided up by a binary gender order. His act can appear mad (and bad) because it lies outside the already known. It connects with chaos (the combination of multiple possible orders) to create new intensities. Like the small boy jumping on the bed, he becomes in that moment a different being, experimenting with intensities usually precluded from those marked as belonging in the category "boy."

The final story here, also from my preschool studies, is of Joanne and her friend Tony taking over the new tree house. The tree house can be thought of in architectural terms as a frame:

> The frame separates. It cuts into a milieu or space. This cutting links it to the plane of composition, to the provisional ordering of chaos through the laying down of a grid or order that entraps chaotic shards, chaoid states, to arrest or slow them into a space and a time, a structure and a form where they can affect and be affected by bodies. (Grosz, 2008a: 13)

On this first day of the tree house's appearance up in the big leafy tree, the group of dominant boys immediately claimed it as belonging in the series of spaces that they were able to control—it belonged with the wooden fort and the top of the climbing frame, for example, which were recognized by everyone as their spaces. But the teachers intervened, telling the boys it was not in that series—it was not a boys' only space. In order to convince them of the break in this series they climbed into the treehouse and pointed out to the protesting boys ensconced there, that they were now there and they were girls. The boys climbed down in disgust and returned to their older undisputed territories.

Joanne had often talked to me about her desire to be a member of the dominant boys' group. But she didn't dare to join them when they were in the fort, as they might push her down. And when they did let her play, they almost always positioned her in a position she did not like, of a princess who had to be saved. Only once had they let her be a hero. On this particular morning she adopted her usual strategy of enticing Tony away from the other boys to play with her.

The teachers had declared the tree house open to anyone. Joanne and Tony climbed up the ladder and quickly developed a strategy for making it their own. They dropped tiny bits of sawdust into the eyes of those who were climbing the ladder, who would then fall down crying onto the grass. The teachers were mystified as to what the problem was, since Tony and Joanne, looking down over the tree house railing, looked completely innocent. Then Tony saw me watching, and shrugged, the expression on his face dismissing me as irrelevant. Presumably I was not a teacher and had no power. But when Joanne saw me watching she stopped, seeing herself through my gaze. She called out to me: "We are just cleaning all this sawdust off the floor that the carpenters have left here."

The takeover of the tree house is both pleasurable and dangerous. It is a new framing of space, in which the as-yet-unknown might take place. Their first experiment is to find a way to make it their own, against the declaration that it is for anyone. The teachers' declaration has cleared it for them to use, but also for everyone else. Their pleasure in the strategic takeover is intense. But it is also dangerous as they may well come undone and be positioned as naughty children. But Joanne is prepared for this undoing and forestalls it with a rapid move back into her good girl category. The category thus works, even in the chaos of the new space, as a protective device. It creates a safe striated space inside the smooth space that had opened up.

Through the habitual repeated, molar striations through which the categories boy and girl are made real we might say that the self of the punching boys in George's story both deciphers and reiterates itself through categories that are secured in the act of their take-up. The self of

Joanne as girl deciphers and reiterates itself in the virtuous act of cleaning the floor. This does not mean she loses the earlier intensities any more than George loses the moment of power in the flight down the slope. Deleuze emphasizes the importance of AND between each of our repetitions and becomings. We are this AND that, always becoming something more, something else. The self is performed through habitual repetitions that may foreclose the new, making the new virtually impossible. Lines of flight, one's own and those of others, can be terrifying and they can be very exciting—and they can be a provocation that generates new intensities and new becomings. I want to suggest here that it is precisely in engaging with the incomprehensible, in going beyond the already-known, and working with it rather than against it, that relationality and community, and becoming-artistic in relation to others, both human and not, can flourish.

The different location of the individual in relation to space and relationality that we explore in this book, has strong ethical implications for one's relations with others and one's relations with place. Ethics no longer rests so much on individualized decision-making subjects, but on the ongoing openness of each to the other, and the recognition each bestows on the other, moment-by-moment. In Braidotti's words, this generates a sustainable ethics through an "enlarged sense of community" responsive to both human and non-human others:

> A sustainable ethics for a non-unitary subject proposes an enlarged sense of interconnection between self and others, including the non-human or 'earth' others, but removing the obstacle of self-centered individualism. This is not the same as absolute loss of values, it rather implies a new way of combining self-interests with the well-being of an enlarged sense of community, which includes one's territorial or environmental interconnections. (Braidotti, 2006: 35)

In Rinaldi's words: "When you consider others as part of your own identity, then their different, sometimes divergent, theories and opinions are seen as a resource. The awareness of the value of these differences and of having dialogue among them increases" (2006: 206).

The individualized and unitary subject, once a significant and desired end-product of educational practices, gives way in this new way of thinking about pedagogy and place, to what Guattari et al. (1995) called an interdependent "'ethico-aesthetic' paradigm," which brings relational "pragmatics and micro-politics" together with "attempts to free expression to create new combinations" (Roy, 2004: 309).

Throughout this book we explore pedagogical relations, including those where art making, writing and theatre are used to create new combinations and possibilities for becoming in contexts where ethics and aesthetics are closely intertwined. The sustainable ethics that Braidotti envisages is generated in these spaces, in part, through the enlargement, expansion and expression made possible in aesthetic and creative practices, and in part through a different kind of attention to relationality.

Ceppi and Zini adopt the term "rich normality" or "dynamic normality" to describe "an environment and a society that are made up of exceptions and special cases... This does not mean adherence to formal or pre-defined parameters, but the conscious and capable management of contradictions and conflicts" (1998: n.p.). This is a very different relationality to that imposed by neoliberalism, where highly individualized subjects compete for limited resources while the technologies of government work on them as a population to become productive (Foucault, 2003). As a population subjected to those technologies, individuals become generic subjects whose best interest is served by being competitive at the expense of others, and by following rules intended to protect those who govern them from risk. In the ethico-aesthetic paradigm, in contrast, individuals have good reason to listen to each other, to care for each other, and to be enlarged by others' difference.

Deleuze and Guattari invite us to generate an amplitude of life, an ethical life, a life not limited by the already known. The concept of the "sovereign individual," alone in his or her power to affect the world, is less significant than the practices that maximize the:

> ...capacities of all bodies to affect and be affected. [Ethics] is also about affirming difference and the production of the new. Rather than limiting the future to what has already been or to what is already known, ethics involves opening up the potential for the unknown. (Hickey-Moody and Malins, 2007: 4)

This openness to the unknown is integral to the spaces of learning that are explored in this book, where relationality and sensitivity to the other (including non-human others) can sometimes transcend the constraints and dictates of curriculum. Ethico-aesthetic connections do not take place in a neutral space. Bodies enfold space and they fold out into space, and are in this sense co-extensive with the places and spaces they inhabit. In Merleau Ponty's terms: "the bodies of others are not objects; they are phenomena that are coextensive with one's own body" (1964:118). Or Weiss: "the experience of being embodied is never a private affair, but is always already mediated by our continual interactions with other human and non-human bodies" (1999: 5). Massey analyses spaces and places as always made up of multiple stories-so-far, that is, stories told from within differing trajectories with radically different histories. Every story, she suggests, is a story unfolding, a story that will encounter other stories that require something new, not in order to deny or negate the other's (sometimes incommensurable) story, but in order to extend the capacity of oneself, and one's community of others, for becoming.

And so...

Each of the chapters that follows engages in a line of flight from a particular assemblage of authors, concepts, becomings and writings, that enables us to explore how pedagogy and place might be thought productively in terms of opening up spaces of becoming, of encounter, of relationality--spaces that are productive of life. In the next chapter Constance turns to the fieldnotes from her ethnographic study of homeless youth, from which she was inspired to draw during the collective biography workshop at Bombo. Her stories take pedagogical encounters beyond the traditional school walls working with young people who are outside the molar order of everyday schooling.

2

LISTENING TO HOMELESS YOUNG PEOPLE: A STRATEGY OF ATTENTION
CONSTANCE ELLWOOD

This morning, again, different students arrive at the school, two boys: Jason and Ryan. Ryan has taken a tablet which "someone" "gave" him. He doesn't know whether it is an upper or a downer. He is jittery and restless. Instead of the work which Matt, the teacher, has prepared for him, Ryan asks for maths but "not multiplication, something easier." Matt introduces me to Ryan, with the implication that we will work together. Jason jumps in with "what about me?" and I make a gesture indicating "yes, sure."

Both of them are restless. Ryan comes in and out of the room, fooling with Jason, groaning, twisting his body around, rolling his eyes, pulling the hood of his jacket up over his backwards baseball cap, the same way Jason wears it. Jason is playing around with backward speech. His example: thuck fey: they fuck. He speaks it fast and asks me if I can understand. No, I say. Jo is standing in the doorway and he asks her and she says she could understand perfectly as a kid, couldn't do it herself now, but can still understand. He is clearly impressed. The boys also talk about the language police use: Tango, Charlie etc. Jason seems to be inserting as many swearwords into his talk as possible, saying fuck and cunt as often as he can.

I sit down next to him. He has his maths folder open on the desk, with the new worksheets on top. He sniffs and grimaces "I stink don't I? I need deodorant don't I? Do I stink? I really stink! Phew!" I say, "I can't smell anything except tobacco." "Tobacco! Huh." His tone implies that I am an idiot, naïve, not a knower of the world. I should have known that it was something else. But I genuinely can only smell tobacco. He jumps up. "I'm going to buy deodorant!" His unbegun worksheet is still on the desk and he's gone for about ten minutes, coming back with a plastic bag containing a spray deodorant, a bottle of Pepsi, and three chocolate bars. He sprays the deodorant all over his clothes on the outside, with a quick spray up the underside of his sloppy joe. I am eyeing off the chocolate bars, wondering whether he will offer them around. Matt jokes with him that he has kindly gone off and bought us all chocolate. Jason is not fazed. He says a whole bag of chocolates was six bucks, too expensive. He doesn't share his chocolate bars.

    He is sitting beside me but doing a lot of other things as well. He is wearing oversized low-slung baggy jeans with monster pockets. At one point he is fiddling with something in one pocket. He asks, "Did you see what was in my pocket?" I say "No." "That's good," he replies and immediately, from his pocket, pulls out and promptly puts back, what looks like a joint rolled in cigarette papers. He regularly stands up to hoist his jeans back to waist-level before sitting down again. His hood obscures his face and he peers out in a kind of concealed way. At one point when he readjusts the hood of his sloppy joe and his baseball cap combination, I get a glimpse of his shaved head and pallid face. His teeth are yellowed and mottled by drug use.

    He is working on subtraction, for example, 745-736=9. The worksheet shows sums in which the answer is given, but one line in the calculation is missing and has to be completed. He seems to have no conception of number, or of the number line. The difference between, say 30 and 2, is described as "heaps." He works everything out by counting back the spaces on a ruler. This gets difficult with numbers that are higher than 30, off the end of the ruler. "My head is hurting," he moans. At first I am confused because he is using a different system of subtraction than the one I learned. My head hurts too as I struggle to get into alignment with this different approach. And also I find it difficult to figure out how to explain it, since it is so simple. At one point I get on a roll when I figure I can explain it in terms of "tens" and "units." This latter word he supplies when I hesitate, unsure of how to describe that column. But this system stops working when we get into a different shaped problem. Again I can't figure out how to explain it.

    I juggle the fragile balance of my roles with him. I am enthusiastic when he gets the answer: "Yep. You got it!" I struggle with the task: "I don't understand. Why is this little number here? AAGGH My head is hurting." I tease him when he's close to the answer: "Hey man! What are you doing? Look what you did here. Why don't you do that again?" I am overwhelmed by the difficulty: "I don't know. I don't know how to do this." I push him to keep going: "Come on just one more! Look! You're nearly at the end of the page!" And I try to participate less and less: "You do it. I'm not doing it. You got the last one right. You do it." Throughout, he is restless, leaving the room for cigarettes, arguing with

Ryan or Matt, putting his head on his arms, scratching himself, moaning, "This'll kill me. This is shit. What are you doing to me? I've had it." When he's on the final page, he leaps up saying "I'm leaving" but comes face-to-face with the whiteboard and begins doing the next problem there. He finishes the final questions on the whiteboard, with me the cheering coach on the sidelines. Ryan, still jittery, comes in when Jason is on the second last problem, "Come on man, let's go! We gotta go. Hurry up man!" Jason ignores him, keeps working, and finishes the worksheet.[i]

This story is based on field notes written while I was carrying out research at Oasis, a school for homeless young people. I attended the school one morning a week over an eight-month period both as a participant observer for a research project into schooling for school refusers, and I offered literacy/numeracy support to whichever students turned up that day. Subsequently, I carried out interviews with five young people[ii] and their teacher. In what follows, I reflect on the research data—field notes and interview comments—in light of the framework offered by Ceppi and Zini (1998). This framework foregrounds "a strategy of attention," or "the willingness to listen and be open to others which is fundamental to any educational context" and which, above all, "creates an empathetic context for listening to [young people] and their hundred languages" (Ceppi and Zini, 1998: n.p.).

I want to show, in this context of a school for homeless young people, what is meant by a strategy of attention, and the ways in which it is fundamental to productive relationships between teachers and students. While this is relevant for all students, my focus is on those so-called 'at-risk' students who have fallen through the gaps in mainstream schooling. For these students, the possibilities of Deleuzian 'differenciation', where subjects are understood as continually engaged in processes of becoming different from themselves, as continuously folding into new possibilities, are particularly potent. The strategy of attention taken up in this chapter refers specifically to attention to 'difference' not as categorical difference, but as openness to non-standard, normative ways of being. It involves:

> A 'pedagogy of listening'—listening to thought—...an ethics of encounter built on welcoming and hospitality of the Other—an openness to the difference of the Other, to the coming of the other. It involves an ethical relationship of openness to the Other, trying to listen to the Other from his or her own position and experience and not treating the Other as the same. The implications are seismic for education. (Dahlberg and Moss, 2006: 15)

A strategy of attention here involves a willingness be open to the diversity of expression—the "hundred languages"—through which students express themselves and their knowledges. These "languages" include their desires, dress, use of expletives, and the role of drugs in their lives. This strategy of attention enables differenciation, in the sense outlined in Chapter One, as an entry into the art of becoming. The metaphor of one hundred languages refers not only to a capability for "a hundred, a thousand creative and communicative potentials" (Rinaldi, 2006: 175) but also to the ways in which recognition, or the making intelligible, of the Other brings them into being (Butler, 2004). I argue that an attention to and respect for students' "hundred languages" not only creates and maintains a necessary sense of relationality and community in Ceppi's and Zini's sense of community but also enables an unfolding, an artful becoming that makes becoming-student possible. For teachers too, a strategy of attention enables a moving-beyond the boundaries of the sedimented self into an openness to difference and to the Other.

Schooling at Oasis

The school was part of the Oasis Youth Network,[iii] a complex of services for homeless youth, run by the Salvation Army in inner city Sydney, Australia. These services included a film making unit, a counseling unit, a girls' club, a work-for-the-dole project and temporary accommodation for about eight young people. The student population of the school was drawn from those staying in this accommodation as well as students who had dropped out of mainstream schooling, were over the age of 16, and who, having heard of Oasis by word-of-mouth, applied to be enrolled. This latter group can also be regarded as homeless in that there had been a history of family breakdown, requiring them to live in refuges or accommodation provided through charitable organizations.

The school itself consisted, at the time of the research, of two classrooms within this larger complex of buildings and programs. One classroom was for students working towards the Year 10 school certificate and the other for those who had not yet achieved that status. This second room—in which my observations were made—functioned to assess the students' educational achievements thus far, including their capacity to participate in learning through a mastery of aspects of schooling normally taken for granted: the capacity to sit still for long periods, the capacity to turn up on time, the capacity for regularity and perseverance, and so on.

Each student at Oasis is supplied with a folder for each of the subjects she or he has elected to begin with, usually Maths or English, as these are compulsory. In this folder are filed the distance education learning materials (for the Year 10 students) or assorted worksheets. Students work on these at their own pace. Since students are likely to be working at different levels in different subjects and at different rates, there is no class group in the mainstream sense. This system has a practical function; since students' attendance is erratic, it ensures that there is always work there for them to do if they do turn up. It is also a strategy instigated by Jo, the main teacher, to discourage competition between the students. The flipside of competition—the failure to achieve—is pre-empted here by steering students away from further experiences of failure which have already figured strongly in their lives. If someone is best, someone must by definition be worst, and such categories are not helpful to homeless young people.

The school provides a relational space in which students work, but it is a relational space of a particular kind. For a number of reasons, the school may not at first be recognizable as a community, as Jason's lack of interest in sharing his chocolate bars may indicate: students work individually, not as a group; some students attend only irregularly; friendships among students may be intense, or they may be fleeting and reiterate the betrayals which have already marked their lives. Yet, in the world of the homeless young person, community and relationality still figure in important ways. The Oasis school opens possibilities for these young people for movement, invention and the constitution of new ways of being in the world.

"Community" is one of the metaphors which describe the characteristics of a desirable educational environment (Ceppi and Zini, 1998). It is characterized as, for example, "a sense of empathy," "a sense of sharing," "conviviality," "a sense of belonging for all those involved" and "a quality of the space that fosters encounters, exchange, empathy, and reciprocity" (Ceppi and Zini, 1998: n.p.). Ceppi and Zini suggest that, in the Reggio Emilia context, this community can be brought about through the active and joint participation of three protagonists: children, teachers and parents. Their inclusion of parents as one of the three protagonists who play a central role in the social system of the school is a major limitation in the possibilities for homeless young people since it is precisely parents who are usually not available to support their children in their educational endeavors.

On the other hand, the molar striations of neoliberal schooling, as described in the Introduction, in which both teachers and students are often positioned as powerless to create anything new and different, is not so dominant at Oasis. Mainstream schooling has been rejected by the young people at Oasis, and it is vital that the approach to teaching does not replicate that which has failed them.

Schooling as usual?

The constraints on teachers and students taking up central or pro-active roles in their own classrooms has been demonstrated in a recent study of Plains High (a pseudonym), a high school located in an outer suburb of Sydney, Australia (Youdell, 2006). The data from Youdell's study provides an example of the ways relationality and community can break down in mainstream high school classrooms where the hundred languages of students cannot be heard or tolerated. The teachers work to accomplish a normative, idealized place, in which the teachers' authority is recognized and the students are positioned, and position themselves, as co-operative within the normative discourses through which the teacher establishes the order of her classroom (Davies and Hunt, 1994). There are strong parallels between moments in the stories of the students I interviewed at Oasis, and the acts of the students in Youdell's data. My research is also situated in Sydney. Youdell's study provides a contextual background, offering rich ethnographic description of everyday practices in mainstream classrooms just like those once attended by the Oasis students, and from which they had been thoroughly abjected through being expelled. There is a commonality of disruptive classroom behaviors that can be seen in both studies, although, as I will discuss, the behaviors and the outcomes for the Oasis students were more severe than for other students.

In the process of creating normative classrooms, in which good teaching can be recognized as taking place, it may be confronting for the teacher to allow students to deviate from normative behavior. In Youdell's data, we see classrooms in which teachers struggle with the behavior of students that lies outside the norms of relationality, that cannot be recognized. The teacher's attention is not on listening but on the need for normative behaviors. Youdell (2006: 91) describes, for example, a class of 14–15 year olds as "chaotic as usual, with limited work either being given by the teacher or undertaken by the students." Two boys, Phil and Trent, are wrestling. The teacher tells them to stop and to sit down but the boys appear to ignore her and then chase each other around the room, accompanying their wrestling and boxing with insults: "Fucking homeless cunt!" "Gutterboy!" "Yeah, piss on him!" The teacher's final intervention is to send one boy out of the classroom. She follows him out and her admonishment can be heard inside the classroom. He returns, "smirking."

The teacher's intervention, sending the boy outside the classroom and loudly admonishing him, can be described not only as an attempt to establish a normative classroom order, but also as abjecting him, casting out the offending part. Abjection, a constitutive process of the "I" and the "not-I" can involve both the rejection of that which is offensive *in* the other—and by extension—the rejection *of* the other him or herself, as well as a simple failure to "recognize" the other, constituting him or her as "beyond" or "outside" the possibilities of recognition (Butler, 2004). The boy is constituted as "unintelligible," or not properly human, because he is operating outside the norms of behavior that the teacher can accept. When students fail to conform to norms of behavior, for whatever reason, the school system has few resources for recognizing either the lines of force behind the lack of conformity or the students themselves (Davies and Hunt, 1994).

The "failure to recognize the Other" appears again and again in Youdell's data. In another section, she discusses a similarly noisy class— "a lot of noise and many students are chatting and joking together" (Youdell, 2006: 111)—in which a disturbing interaction takes place between a teacher and a student, Julie. The students, again aged 14–15, were working individually on worksheets:

> JULIE: Miss?
> MISS STARKEY *is standing close enough to hear her, but makes no response.*
> JULIE (shouting): MISS!
> *Again, the teacher does not respond.*
> JULIE: Don't ignore me, BITCH!
> *Miss Starkey looks up at Julie.*
> STUDENT SEATED NEARBY: *Did she just say 'bitch'?!*
> JULIE: Yeah, well you ARE a bitch, aren't you, bitch?
> *Miss Starkey gives Julie a disapproving glance, but goes on with what she is doing. Ten minutes later, Julie is still working on her worksheet.*
> JULIE: Miss? I can't figure out the answer to that one!

> Miss Starkey goes to Julie and helps her with the answer. Once Miss Starkey moves on to someone else, Julie chats with some girls sitting nearby. After that line of conversation finishes, Julie says aloud, to no-one in particular, "I've finished my work for the day!" She commences playing with her hair and chewing her nails. (Youdell, 2006: 111–12)

We are ignorant of the relationship between Julie and the teacher, which may explain the inconsistencies in the teacher's responses, first ignoring Julie then assisting her. Nevertheless, the teacher's initial resistance to acknowledging Julie appears to provoke Julie's inappropriate use of language. In other words, the lack of recognition may indeed provoke the bad behavior. While such verbal abuse is widely regarded as highly reprehensible, a "failure to recognize" is less rarely questioned, yet recognition is a key aspect of a relational community. The "exchange, empathy and reciprocity" of which Ceppi and Zini speak cannot be engendered without it.

In another section of data (Youdell, 2006: 126), a teacher reads aloud against a background of "low-level activity and discussion." One of the boys, Paul, makes "popping noises." The teacher is bothered and objects. Paul apologizes but continues to be restless "fidgeting in his seat, tapping his fingers on his desk." When Paul stands up and leans against the window behind his chair, the teacher objects again. The result of the ensuing stand-off is that, after being told to stand outside the classroom door, Paul appears to walk off across the quadrangle outside the classroom. At this point, the remaining students become more engaged in the event. They call out comments, including "You're losing him Miss!" The teacher appears to ignore these comments and continues reading. "A few minutes later Paul returns to the door of the classroom, he stands at the window of the closed door, looking in and grinning and making faces at students in the classroom."

In these extracts, the teachers constitute the problem students as unintelligible, unrecognizable and outside the norms of relationality. Whatever it is that is being expressed through Paul's popping noises and fidgeting is not investigated and remains unknown; whatever is behind Phil's and Trent's fighting and mutual accusations of homelessness is given no place. And it is oddly relevant for this chapter that "homelessness" has become here a term of abuse. Without further investigation, we cannot know whether one or both of these boys are already homeless, are referring to its imminent possibility, or are merely aware of the stigma homelessness entails.

No attempt is made in this classroom to translate or interpret whatever is being expressed through the "hundred languages" of the Other. There is a lack of relationality in the teachers' "lack of recognition" and the students reiterate this in their isolated behavior—for example, Julie talks to "no-one in particular" (Youdell, 2006: 112)—and in their abusive behavior towards the teacher and each other. The teachers' lack of response or acknowledgement takes the form of disapproving glances, reprobation or abjection. The teachers' refusals to interact and, in particular, Miss Starkey's warning to Phil which takes place outside the classroom, seem to indicate a desire to keep the classroom space untainted by the "negativity" of reprobation. However, not only does Miss Starkey's attempt fail, since it can be overheard from within the classroom, but this tendency to separate types of interactions seems to be part of an attempt to maintain an idealized classroom space by abjecting all that does not fit within it. Ideas of community, relationality and respect for difference are absent here. There is no "sense of empathy," no "sense of belonging for all those involved," and above all no "closeness that creates bonds, that enables each group member to recognize the other and to recognize him/herself in the other" (Ceppi and Zini, 1998: n.p.). The teachers' rejections of the students and Julie's derogatory address of Miss Starkey as "bitch" go no way towards "the internalization of the other as a value" (Ceppi and Zini: 1998: n.p.), a crucial aspect of the creation of community.

Additionally, the misbehaving students have been fixed in the category of misbehaver. Miss Starkey's disapproving glances at Julie and the teacher's ongoing problems with Paul indicate that each of these students has already been allocated the static identity of troublemaker, a position beyond which has become increasingly difficult to move.

To an observer, the students appear continually to have the upper hand: Phil's smirk as he returns to the classroom would be read by the other students as a continuing resistance to the teacher's demands to behave, and Paul's antics outside the room confirm his capacity to disrupt, as well as the fact that not only has the teacher "lost" Paul, as the other students have already pointed out, but also, and consequently, that she loses the attention of the whole class. Yet these momentary acts of power, as any teacher knows, sell the students short; they are increasingly excluded from the possibilities which education should provide (DSF, 2007; Sweet, 2006).

Students at Oasis

There are strong parallels between the experiences of these Plains High students and the Oasis students' experiences of mainstream school contexts, particularly in terms of being positioned as unintelligible and as Other to the norms of schooling. In most cases, the Oasis students had been expelled—abjected—following the physical assault of teachers and other direct forms of disobedience such as smoking marijuana on school premises. Jaydana told me that she had been expelled at the age of 14, because "I assaulted one of the teachers after he pushed me...I said 'could I go to the bathroom?' and he said I could, and then when I went to leave the classroom, he pushed me back into it...I picked up a chair and threw it at him and then smashed two windows and threw a computer at him, computer monitor...he was an arsehole of a teacher and he didn't like me very much." Another student, Nicole, described one of her previous schools as having "teachers [who] are out to get you." She illustrated this with the following story: "I used to get afternoon detentions for things I hadn't even done...I was working in the school canteen, at a course thing, little course thing and I was just working in there, and my friends were having a fight outside, and I walked out there to see what was going on, they were fighting, I walked away, and I got an afternoon detention for harassment."

For these students, life at school was marked by acts of behavior regarded as wild, inappropriate, beyond the boundaries of normality, and their teachers' responses suggest that these acts of behavior were, usually, incomprehensible to them. However, behind these wild and apparently incomprehensible acts were histories which, once they are known, make this behavior entirely comprehensible. The students themselves understood this. Jaydana, for example, was aware of her own contribution to the situation: "I was a bit of head case back in that day...I had quite a few issues going on and wasn't dealing with them." Like Jaydana, Nicole was aware that teachers "picked on" her because "I was a bit off the rails." Another student, Kelvin, who was also expelled, at 14, for throwing a chair, explained his behavior as a direct result of an unfeeling comment by a teacher: "She said my parents didn't love me, the way I act proves that my parents don't love me."

Knowing the history of each student's home life experiences allows us to make some sense of what tends to be seen as unintelligible. Rather than having had a stable homelife in the care of a nuclear family, the students at Oasis had, for most of their lives, been apart from their natural parents, and had lived in a series of different homes, none of which appeared to provide the stability needed for a regular and applied focus on schoolwork.

Disrupted homelife experiences were common to all the students I interviewed at Oasis. Jaydana described herself as "running amok" at school because of "living arrangements, my parents, things going on in my life." She described finding places to sleep at night "here there and everywhere." Nicole, after an argument with her aunt over being blamed for her cousin's misdemeanors, had moved to live with her father and his brothers, Nicole's uncles. However, as Nicole commented matter-of-factly: "My dad is a heroin addict. So are my uncles, and they are all using and it wasn't the best environment for a 14-year-old...then one day, like, stuff happened between me and my uncle and I ended up getting an AVO[iv] out on him and then my family turned their back, or that side of my family didn't want anything to do with me." Both Brooke and Kelvin had been raised in foster homes from the age of three and both had had negative experiences in those "homes." Kelvin described the final one, after a series of temporary placements, as a place in which "I would always get the fucking shit kicked out of me every day, and fucking who cares if it is a stable house, I would rather sleep on the streets and not get the shit beat out of me all the time...my foster mum, she used to beat the shit out of me and DOCS[v] are trying to tell me that that house is better." At 15, he moved out onto the streets, "I just figured one day 'fuck this' I don't need to live here anymore, I'm old enough to move out." Brooke, similarly, was with a series of foster families. She described the experience as "Not what a lot of people expect it to be. A lot of people expect foster families to be good and caring but in my first one there was a lot of domestic violence and stuff and unfair treatment...and in the second one it was kind of the same. To me it felt like they were treating their kids better than me and that made me feel unfair and that sort of stuff, so it used to get to my head a little bit...I wasn't allowed out certain times but their kids were allowed out whenever they wanted to, that sort of stuff, just made me feel a bit more unfair, like they were just not worrying, just treating me differently...just if I would get in trouble I would get hit pretty seriously or hit with something by the foster parent...and the daughter would hit me too if she wanted to." Like Kelvin and Nicole, Brooke decided that living in refuges or on the street was a better option than these "homes" which were not homes.

Pedagogy of listening

Clearly, not every misbehaving school student will end up on the streets. However, there are definite parallels between the acts of refusal by both groups of students to participate in the educational and disciplinary systems of mainstream schools. What is important to consider is that sense can always be made of a student's behavior. A strategy of attention, a pedagogy of listening, plays a key role here.

Strategy of attention is about listening with more than the ears to the thousand ways in which we, and others, express ourselves and communicate. It is, among other things, about "welcoming and being open to differences, recognising the value of the other's point of view and interpretation"; it is "an active verb that involves interpretation, giving meaning to the message and value to those who offer it"; "it requires a suspension of our judgements and above all our prejudices" (Rinaldi, 2006: 65). When we activate "a strategy of attention," students' behaviors come to make sense. Rather than seeing a student as unintelligible and unrecognizable, an approach which seeks to know something of the Other—to know something of the students' "hundred languages"— provides the doorway into relationality. What kinds of relationality were provided at the school at Oasis?

The school was a place to which students could come and go as they pleased. They were free to leave the classroom for a cigarette and to work at their own pace. There were no bells and no timetables, no assemblies and no detentions. This free movement around, in, and to the classroom space replaces the striated and hierarchical space of the mainstream classroom described earlier with a smooth space, which facilitates the becoming of something other. Space here is active, physical and relational. It provides a second skin for the possibilities of change, in combination with a focus on a strategy of attention.

Jo, the main teacher, appeared to epitomize this strategy of attention and to recognize this as a key to relationality and the building of a community which could support the personal and educational growth of these students. Indeed, when I asked, in the interviews, "What is different about this school?" the answer was a unanimous: "Jo."

Jo had been a full-time teacher at the school for eight years and was deeply committed to it and the students. An initial volunteer role with the Salvation Army had brought her into contact with the young people and had drawn attention to the impossibility of their situation: "they were antisocial and they were well behind everybody else...they were on drugs." Since at that time there were no schools open to them, she saw that the young people had no possibility of continuing their education. However, with appropriate attention and responsive pedagogy, she recognized that they had the capacity to achieve. After requesting support for a school from the director of the Oasis Youth Network, Jo had enrolled in and completed a three-year teaching qualification and had subsequently opened the school. While Jo had also come from a family oriented to the needs of others, it seems that Jo's willingness to be affected by others and to act on that affect is crucial to her successful enactment of a strategy of attention. This could be seen in her ongoing associations with many ex-students and in the comments of the current students.

One key way in which Jo was described was as a listener, as someone who had time for each student. Kelvin said: "She's not like other teachers she actually cares and wants to listen to something you have to say, she doesn't just tell you no I'm too busy no I'm too busy no I'm too busy...like other teachers...she's understanding; she cares." Jaydana stressed that "you know, I sit down and I tell her what is going on in my life and she understands on an extent, you know, why I am the way I am now because of what has gone on, she is a really understanding lady." Mick also reinforced her availability to students who need her: "She's always got time for you...Jo will never say, oh no I'm too busy." These comments from students verify "the willingness to listen and be open to others which is fundamental to any educational context." This is the "strategy of attention" called for by Ceppi and Zini (1998: n.p.). For the young people at Oasis, new life emerged from the flows and intensities of these moment to moment encounters.

Related to this, the students valued the one-to-one help with schoolwork that was available at Oasis. This one-to-one attention is often not possible in mainstream schooling with larger class sizes and a time- and outcome-oriented curriculum. However, for students with a history of failure and compromised schooling this appears to be a crucial contributor towards their success. Again, this aspect of the context created possibilities for opening the space to enable change. Brooke explained: "She will sit down with you, explain the work to you, help you find the answer, but at the same time, show you how to get the answer yourself. And she will help you if you are wrong, like she will help you try and correct the answer and it is really good, like, it is easy because I can talk to her easily about it and I don't have to worry about the rest of the class, having to have her at the same time…I didn't feel like that at [mainstream] school. Nicole elaborated that: "She is very patient with us and like helps as much as she can and if you don't understand something she will go through it different ways until you do understand it." Students' difficulties in understanding some of the schoolwork and their desires to master the task are both recognized here, and accommodated.

Jo also provided recognition in the form of an alertness to the presence of drugs or alcohol in the students. Jaydana commented that "I try not to come to school stoned, because I know Jo doesn't like it, and I find it—I think it's disrespectful…I don't like, I see the way Jo looks at me when I'm stoned and the way she talks to me and then when I'm straight and sober, like, she is different, you know what I mean?"

In the face of her knowledge and understanding of the young people's use of drugs and alcohol, Jo was pragmatic. She advised me, for example, never to bring any valuables to the school. "The kids have drug habits and need to support those habits, therefore they must steal." If I had something stolen, I could only blame myself, she said. Yet, the students' drug habits did not prejudice Jo against them. As Jaydana said, Jo always saw the positive in the students: "she doesn't try and make you feel bad about anything, or she is always looking for the positives. She never sees the bad in anyone, she always sees the good. That's what we need around here, we need more people that can see the good in the kids around here because we aren't perfect little angels." In going beyond the usual differences of race, religion, sex, and culture, to the challenging differences engendered through drug use, Jo demonstrated "respect for differences, however they may be expressed" and an "internalisation of the other as a value" (Ceppi and Zini, 1998: n.p.). Inherent in this stance, she maintained a view of the students as subjects open to becoming different from themselves.

Jo's actions also conform to Ceppi's and Zini's suggestion that "the space [be] given shape and identity by the relationships created within it" (1998: n.p.). In my field notes, I observed that Jo worked to keep the space as one which was dedicated to learning. "As I wait, I stand in the doorway [of the main school room] and after some time notice that on the couch in the little adjoining room there is a boy curled in a foetal position regarding me. He looks flushed and as if he is not well, recuperating from something. He is slight of build. I ask him if he knows where Jo is and he answers politely that he doesn't. A little later, Jo returns and sees the boy there. She goes immediately towards him, saying "No, this is not the place. You can't sleep here. No, move away from here. No, this is not right. You can't do that here." He protests weakly and leaves for the open courtyard outside, looking hangdog. Jo explains to me that he has "a big problem with alcohol." This pallid boy turned out to be Kelvin, who later in the day was one of my interviewees.

Unlike Youdell's teacher who abjects the misbehaving boy from the classroom, there is a different quality to Jo's pressure on Kelvin to leave the space and this is reflected in his comment in the interview that "Jo is probably the best teacher I've had." Jo's focus on guarding this classroom space as a pedagogical space can be seen in her matter-of-fact definition: "No, this is not the place" and in her reiteration of the word "here." She defines what is right or wrong for this particular space, rather than accusing Kelvin of bad behavior. Additionally, however, an already-established relationality enables Kelvin to recognize the strategy of care in Jo's intentions. The students themselves are aware of this defense of the space for pedagogical purposes and know that its goal is to support their transition out of drugs and into educational gain.

Jo also managed the in-between of the striated and smooth spaces. By offering a space which was structured and organized, and for which there were some ground rules—"don't come if you are stoned," she made available a smooth space "in which movement is less regulated or controlled, and where bodies can interact—and transform themselves—in endlessly different ways" (Hickey-Moody and Malins, 2007: 11). In contrast to the overriding striations of schooling in which the constraints on change are paramount, the classroom at Oasis created an environment of "dynamic normality" (Ceppi and Zini, 1998: n.p.) with the possibility of differenciation. Here, changes could take place within a system of respect for difference and without notions of an Other who must be abjected. Both in her defense of the space, and in her capacities for a positive relationality through listening, understanding and respect, Jo created a different kind of space, one in which connections between teacher and student were enabled, schoolwork was attended to, and "the hundred languages" of these students could be heard and understood.

The behavior of many homeless young people can be viewed as so far beyond the bounds of what is considered normal as to be irreparable, and the young people themselves are often seen as irredeemable. The previous discussion demonstrates how a strategy of attention—as respect for diversity and as recognition of the other—makes these at-risk young people intelligible and no longer irredeemable. This strategy of attention was seen in Jo's encounters with the students but not between teachers and students in Youdell's study. If teachers are to make a difference to the lives of their students, it is crucial that they have the capacity to enact a strategy of attention, and to thereby enable change. This is an ethical pedagogy wherein students are no longer trapped in the already known but openings are created for movement and invention. Paul Moulds, the Director of Oasis, suggests that an attitude involving "offering" is required for change: "if you keep offering, a window of opportunity opens" (ABC online forum, 2008). Yet, what does it mean to "offer"? And how can spaces be opened for becomings to take place?

In order to make sense of individual capacities to enact and enable a strategy of attention, I turn now to elucidate the ways in which a strategy of attention enables a movement beyond the boundaries of the sedimented self. My focus here is on "becoming" in teachers. I speak from a position that views the capacity for a strategy of attention in teachers as playing a crucial role in the "becomings" of students. As Deleuze says, teaching is about enabling a *moving with*. He says, "we learn nothing from those who say 'do as I do'. Our only teachers are those who tell us to 'do with me'" (Deleuze, 1994: 23). Learning, for teachers and students, is movement in relation. It is heterogeneous, emerging in the interplay of sign and response in the intimacy of the pedagogical encounter, in the "encounter with the Other" (Deleuze, 1994: 22). In a Deleuzian pedagogy, it is important to find ways to enable all teachers to expand their capacities for *moving with* others.

What forces us to think creatively and to move beyond the boundaries of our current habituated thought is "an object not of recognition but of a fundamental *encounter*" (Deleuze, 1994, p. 139). While "an object of recognition" is something known, since only the known is recognizable, a fundamental encounter involves an openness to the haecceity of the other. The term haecceity refers to "degrees of power which combine, to which correspond a power to affect and be affected, active or passive effects, intensities" (Deleuze and Parnet, 2002: 92). They are thus events, moments in which encounters occur and the possibility of new thinking can occur. Such new thinking affirms life and means "discovering, inventing, new possibilities of life" (Deleuze, 1983: 101).

The concept of a strategy of attention relies on a Deleuzian notion of difference as pure event, pure intensity. That is, difference as I discuss it here is not based on "difference *from* or *within* something" (Foucault, 1977: 181-2). It is not solely a process in which one listens well to the other, with attention and good will, and accepts the validity of the other on the basis of a conscious process of positive evaluation. This kind of listening, locked into the already known, is not capable of breaking the boundaries of habituated concepts. Rather, in the Deleuzian concept of difference, a strategy of attention is an experience of sensing rather than conceiving; it "moves the soul" (Deleuze, 1994: 140); it involves intensities; it apprehends. It means becoming "capable of loving, without remembering, without phantasm, and without interpretation, without taking stock" (Deleuze and Parnet, 2002: 47). It is such encounters that I want to consider here, through a reflection on my own differenciation—my own processes of opening to difference—as teacher/researcher undertaking this research project.

Differenciation

I take myself as a case study here for two reasons. First, like the teachers in Youdell's study, and like all teachers, I am equally capable of failing to employ a strategy of attention, particularly in a complex teaching space with its multiple conflicting demands. Second, the event which I relate below slipped smoothly into the flow of this research study, illustrating not only "affirming chance" (Deleuze, 1994: 200) but also the importance of the capacity for connection and the becoming which is the outcome of such connection.

In undertaking this research, I was exposed to a site and actors within it which were radically different from anything I had experienced previously. Although I had taught for many years, I had had no previous contact with homeless young people. Before being accepted as a researcher, it was politely suggested that I do a training course run by the Salvation Army, *Introduction to Youth Homelessness*. Many of my fellow students on the course were ex-homeless, ex-drug users and ex-prisoners. My exposure to them began a process of differenciation as I experienced myself as being in the default position proposed by Latour, "always one reflexive loop *behind*" (2005: 33).

One evening, we addressed the topic of diverse responses to drugs, such as heroin and ice (crystal methamphetamine). The next day, when travelling home from work, I had a synchronistic encounter with a young man on a train. The following story was written in my journal the day after this encounter.

I get on the train with my bike and sit in the end section of the carriage. Opposite me is a young man, wearing very dark wraparound sunglasses and a bandanna tied tightly around his smooth-skulled head. One leg jiggles incessantly and some tattoos are visible on his biceps and shoulders, which show signs of having worked out in a gym. His face is impassive and, apart from the jiggling leg, he is relatively unmoving and stares directly ahead. Any movements he makes to look out the window, for example, are unusually slow and deliberate. Unnervingly, he appears to be staring at me since I am sitting opposite him.

I understand instantly that drugs are involved here, in some way. I notice the connective glances of some other passengers, as they look at him through the window from the platform, their jittery step and drooping eyes indicating their own drug use. The sense of recognition and interconnection in their faces confirms my understanding that drug users can sense out each other and are instantly connected, this understanding a product of my own single case of experimentation with LSD in the 1970s. Given the young man's lack of movement and lack of activity, only his stillness and impassive stare could have provided them with the signals.

But after the previous evening's lecture, my curiosity is aroused. I have a strong desire to know more about him. This curiosity is in contrast to what I believe would have been my previous response: fearful and very alert to possible danger. In the past, without the bike, I would have immediately moved, probably to the supposedly safe refuge of the carriage with the blue light, to a seat which enabled the best view of potential dangers and the quickest escape. With the bike, I would have remained doubly alert, perhaps even getting off and waiting for the next train if I thought I was at risk.

Nevertheless I hate being stared at. When the person sitting on the young man's stretch of seats leaves, I get up and move to sit on the same side as him. There are about three or four seat spaces between us. From this position, I continue to watch him in the reflection of the windows opposite.

We travel thus for some time. For me, it is a 40-minute trip, terminating in the city, at Central Station. I am plugged in, listening to my iPod, but the volume isn't loud, and when he turns and asks me a question, I hear it well enough.

He turns from the waist, in that slow and deliberate way, leans towards me and asks, in a broad Australian accent with its characteristic slurring and dipthongs, and articulating each word with effort, "Excuse me. Is this the train to Long Bay Jail?"

Long Bay Jail is a men's prison, situated on the eastern-most promontory of Botany Bay. In terms of public transport, it is accessible only by bus, a long trip which departs from Central Station, in a direction roughly opposite to the one from which we are coming. We certainly are not on the train to Long Bay Jail.

My own experience of Long Bay Jail comes from a time, long past, when I was employed to teach Creative Writing there. I was completely unnerved and undone in that environment. The sense of being locked in at the heart of so many walls, with so many thick gates, and large keys, watched over by apparently unfeeling prison guards, and with prisoners themselves padding silently up behind me, their breath on the back of my neck. I was aware at the time that I had never had any brothers, had been to an all-girls' school, and that somehow the rough jocularity of boys and men was a foreign territory to me. At the time, I didn't see that other complexities of my background also made this site strange to me. At the time, I just knew I had to get out and I quit in a state of nervous terror after only three weeks, writing in my journal that I felt like eggshells.

So when the young man leans towards me, with intensity burning in his controlled movements, and his unseeable expression hidden behind the wraparound sunglasses, I experience an ancient tremor of fear. But the content of the evening before is strongly in me. I remove the earbuds of my iPod and say slowly, "No. It doesn't. You have to catch a bus, from Central, at Eddy Avenue. Do you know Eddy Avenue?"

He moves back slowly, to his upright position, making a noncommittal response. I guess that he doesn't know Eddy Avenue, but that he doesn't want to admit that either.

The people sitting opposite watch this interaction with interest, but we disappoint them by continuing no further. However, I am trying to think of a way to continue our conversation.

After a long silence, I ask again about his knowledge of Eddy Avenue. From there we move into an extended conversation which continues after we leave the train and I take him to the buses at Eddy

Avenue. We talk about where he had grown up, who had brought him up, his absent parents, drugs and so on.

He tells me, among other things, about what it is like to be on ice. Really bad, he says. He had been completely paranoid, and had stood in the middle of his bedroom brandishing a cutlass in case of attack. Currently he is on some kind of downer, because he is just out of rehab. He had been brought up by an aunt, both parents being heroin addicts. And he is on his way to visit his father who is in Long Bay Jail "for the last time." I ask how he knows it will be the last time. He says his father has been convicted of a triple homicide, and will certainly be dead before the sentence is up. When I ask him about schooling, he says slowly and with some pride: well I finished Year 7.

The story illustrates both a capacity for a strategy of attention and the way this strategy of attention expands capacities for becoming. As I understand it, the *Youth Homelessness* course and my exposure to the world of the young homeless people opened the possibilities for this encounter on the train which in turn expanded the possibilities for my understanding of the other. A strategy of attention was key to this process. This strategy of attention is a "being with" rather than an attempt to evaluate, name or represent. It is marked by an open curiosity, rather than by a sedimented history featuring old fears—such as my fear of an undifferentiated maleness, violence and drug use—and prejudices—what we "know" and therefore expect of "druggies" and street kids. A strategy of attention lays aside fear and prejudice and replaces them with an openness to the haecceity of the encounter. We are with the speeds and slownesses, the intensities of the other, moment by moment. "Movements, becomings, in other words, pure relations of speed and slowness, pure affects, are below and above the threshold of perception" (Deleuze and Guattari, 1987: 281). Something new happens when the teacher/researcher opens to the flows and intensities of encounter, to moment by moment opportunities for recognition and movement from the already known.

In my encounter with the young man on the train, the speeds and slownesses and intensities of which Deleuze speaks are in evidence. There is a kind of controlled dance in our initial encounter, as I experience fear, openness and curiosity. Subsequently, the encounter normalizes as the conversation turns to information getting. But this too supports the encounter as I hear the details of a life not only different from my own but one which I can only view as disastrous. Yet as I listen, my view is challenged by the normality of its presentation, and by the positives and the achievements. I am aware, in reflection, of the moments when my strategy of attention fails; for example, when he tells me he has only completed Year 7, I find myself full of anxiety on his behalf, wanting to insist that he must do more schooling. Such a "craze for interpretation" (Deleuze and Parnet, 2002: 46), in which we want to find significance in order to make "sense," precludes the liberation of becoming. Both the smooth and the striated are evident in my responses but there has been a differenciation from the time when I felt like "eggshells" to this encounter where I have connected with the other and increased my own potential to become-other with them.

Thus it was, I believe, that I found myself able, during the subsequent research project, to listen calmly to the hundred languages of the young people at Oasis, that I was enabled to encompass the jittery restlessness of someone on "ice," to remain optimistic when confronted by a 19-year-old student who could not count beyond the end of a ruler; and that I was able to suspend previous fears and judgments around drugs, violence and lack of education. A strategy of attention, as an opening to becoming-other through connection, enabled my differenciation here. A strategy of attention, as a capacity to *move with,* was present in my classroom interactions with Jason and the other students. It resulted in an approach to these young people that did not mark off absolute boundaries between myself and them as the other, or between myself as the known and the other as the unknown.

Chapter Three, *Relationality and the art of becoming* by Catherine Camden Pratt, works with the story of Kiet, a child she taught in kindergarten. Catherine explores how art making in community, using Ceppi's and Zini's theorizing of community in place, opens both children and teacher to individual and communal lines of flight. The chapter also examines tensions between smooth and striated space. Although teacher and children hold the molar order of the classroom in place, they simultaneously open possibilities for movement towards the not-yet-known and a new and responsive sense of community. The strategy of attention that has been discussed in this chapter is a key element of the relationality that characterizes the pedagogical encounters in the kindergarten classroom in Chapter Three.

Notes

[i] Most names in this chapter are pseudonyms. Exceptions are the name of the school, and the names of two of the key people at the school: Jo, the main teacher, and Captain Paul Moulds, the Director. Names used with permission.

[ii] These students' ages ranged between 17 and 20. They had all dropped out of mainstream schooling at some time during Year 8 or 9; that is, generally aged around 14 to 16.

[iii] The Oasis Youth Network (not a pseudonym) was the topic of a television documentary screened in early 2008. See: <http://www.abc.net.au/tv/oasis/about/synopsis.htm>.

[iv] Apprehended Violence Order, in which the recipient is banned from approaching the person who has taken out the AVO.

[v] Department of Community Services.

3
RELATIONALITY AND THE ART OF BECOMING
CATHERINE CAMDEN PRATT

In this chapter I reflect on pedagogical moves I took thirteen years ago as a teacher in a state run Kindergarten in a New South Wales Primary School—an institutional setting organized around the planned, orderly production of pre-specified educational outcomes. It is a story of uncertainty, and of tension between controlling molar forces in a classroom, and lines of flight, between striated orderly management of space, and the smooth spaces of the not-yet-known. It is about the art of becoming with a particular focus on art work within a pedagogical community in which group members come to recognize the other and to recognize themselves in the other through making art. It is a story of relationality and the art of becoming.

We become ourselves in and through community while simultaneously co-creating community. In Deleuze's thinking, becoming is both a de-individualizing move in which the individual is able to escape some of his or her limitations, and a move in which the individual differenciates herself, becomes something other than she was—something new. For Ceppi and Zini movement towards the new requires a "strategy of attention" in which there is "openness and attention to others as a value, [and] respect for differences, however they are expressed" (Ceppi and Zini, 1998: 2). As Constance discussed in Chapter Two, this strategy creates a relational space in which teachers and students can listen to "children and their hundred languages" (Ceppi and Zini, 1998: 3). In these ways the classroom community can become a relational space in which and through which teachers and students are open to *differenciation*.

In the story in this chapter, art making in community opens both children and teacher to individual and communal lines of flight. In times of increasingly standardized curricula and quantitative measures of "outcomes," as they currently exist in Australian school curricula, there may be considerable tension between, on the one hand, idiosyncratic moments of differenciation and lines of flight and, on the other, the planned, orderly production of outcomes. For students and teachers, lines of flight enable crucial engagements in the processes of differenciation—

of becoming something other to the already known, the established. A line of flight is not necessarily disruptive, but it is different and unanticipated, and it may be difficult for a teacher to know whether or how to support it; it may even be difficult to read it at all except as disruptive. While all contexts can be interrupted by lines of flight, a teacher cannot plan a line of flight. However a teacher can set up conditions in which lines of flight are made more possible. I am interested in the places where lines of flight are made more possible, and supportable.

This chapter explores a story where the molar order of a classroom functions both as an orderly background enabling and supporting the processes of becoming, and as an order that may be in conflict with a child's line of flight. What emerges in the classroom community from an individual child's line of flight is grounded in and subsequently shapes relationality. The practices of art making in the kindergarten classroom are crucial to this opening to the new and the unknown that enables the children's learning.

When the events told in this story took place, I was a classroom teacher without an art making practice. My experience at that time was limited to some art making as a classroom teacher alongside students and my own in-process drawings that I had done in a therapeutic context as I explored traumatic aspects of my childhood. Today, I have an established art making practice, which emerged in and developed through my PhD research into the legacies of maternal 'madness'. (Camden Pratt, 2002, 2006, 2007; Horsfall et al., 2007).

Art making and the in-between: art making and relationality

As I have explored elsewhere, making art interrupts the linear verbal narrative and invites the art maker into a hyphenated—or in-between—space (Camden Pratt, 2002, 2007, 2008). In this in-between space unknowns swirl and all is in be-coming. Here chaos waits. Working with art takes up and connects with this chaos, and can impacts on the body in ways that enable new knowing (Camden Pratt, 2002, 2007). Art may set out to represent the already known, but it can also set out to find a way to represent that which cannot be said, or heard or seen, because it is not yet known in a way that is re-presentable. As I discovered with art making in my PhD "painting released a voice I did not know I had—I could show what words could not...I did not know what would emerge each time I came to the door sized boards. I painted to know—working the hyphens of myself(s)" (Camden Pratt, 2007: 145, 253).

Talking about art I take on Deleuze's idea that art produces "sensations, affects, intensities as its mode of addressing problems [and is a] system of dynamized and impacting forces rather than a system of unique images that function under the regime of signs" (Grosz, 2008a: 1-3). Those who work with Deleuze are not interested in art that represents the already known, but in art that shifts what it is possible to know. As I found through my own work its materiality, and its connection with chaos—the multiple and conflicting orders out of which we sculpt and forge our everyday lives—potentially lead to a material shift in the body of the artist and potentially of the viewer. Painting specifically "ever more deeply materializes the body" through its relationship with chaotic forces (Grosz, 2008a: 21) and makes visible what was invisible, expresses and explores what cannot be represented. Art is "that which impacts on the body most directly, that which intensifies and affects most viscerally" (Grosz, 2008a: 24). This materiality brings a relational intensity to art making in community. A teacher's strategy of attention to students engaged in art making can support them in connecting with chaos in ways that make something new possible for individuals and communities (Camden Pratt, 2008).

Art making as classroom practice opens up new possibilities for teachers and students (Camden Pratt, 2008; Springgay, 2008). Springgay writes about art making as an emergent pedagogy marked by "relationality, generosity and corporeality" (2008: 122). The particular thisness of artistic production generates pedagogical moments that go beyond the already-known, the planned, or the anticipated and desired end-point. Writing of her own students' art works Springgay locates becoming in the in-between spaces of the making of art where the emphasis is very much "in the making," reminiscent of the emergent play of the children in the sandpit in Chapter One. In Springgay's art class:

> [P]edagogy did not exist prior to these sites (the teachers, students, the art works) rather pedagogy was created, materialized, and mobilized through participation 'in the making'. Pedagogy seeps into the cracks in-between the bodies of the students, in-between their artistic interventions, and in-between the spaces of learning and knowing. This thinking of the in-between of pedagogy presents us with strange and unfamiliar constructs, staging encounters with the unthought, the unknown, and the ambiguous. (Springgay, 2008: 123)

It is in the in-between spaces that lines of flight take off. Art making enables in-between spaces in which lines of flight, of differenciation, of becoming, become possible. The quality of connections is important in this relational space.

The moment stretches out

In this story the children, and me the teacher, together, must deal with the conflict and moment of chaos that opens up between the safely managed, school-approved, orderly classroom, and Kiet—a small girl who opens up a different possibility, who engages in an unexpected line of flight. Kiet's line of flight takes her outside what the children at her table understand to be appropriate practice for their new kindergarten classroom, and for the art making task at hand. Unlike Kiet they are using the rich colored paints, paper and brushes in a more visibly orderly way to engage in the English literacy activity I have set them. However collectively, they use paper and the rich reds, blues, yellows and browns to explore the in-between of leaving home and coming to school to become something new, to become people who are literate in the English language.

Unlike her classmates, Kiet had spent approximately the first three and a half years of her life in an orphanage in Thailand. Since then she had lived in Australia, after being adopted by her Anglo-Australian parents. When she began Kindergarten she was already six, and turned seven during the year, unlike the other children in her class, some of whom would not turn six until the following year.[i]

I tell the story in two parts.

Part 1
Five-year-old voices hum in the air—the children are new to 'big school'. It is morning and the Kindergarten children are engaged with a wide variety of English literacy activities. They work noisily in four small groups using specific materials in inter-related activities exploring their experiences of beginning school. One group draw pictures of how they get to school and I write their stories; another makes little scenes with play-dough showing what they see on their way to school; a third begins to paint the extra large cardboard boxes that will become cubby houses in the classroom and the fourth paints their homes and families. "Miss Camden Pratt" a little hand touches my arm, "Yes?" Georgiy's face

wears a frown. "Come and see what Kiet's doing." We walk across the room to the large painting table. Five children are crammed together at one end: their elbows touching, brushes mid air, faces tightened, their paintings half finished, their eyes on Kiet. Kiet's body bends tightly over the table, alone at the other end, her thin arms angled sharply out from the blue checked sleeves of her new uniform. Her little hands move swiftly across her paper and green-purple paint squishes through her splayed fingers. I stand next to her. Her concentration splashes the table: a soundless waterfall in monsoon rains. We are quiet. The moment stretches out. Kiet's little fingers push silently squishing through the layered thick, now mud-colored paint on her paper, her hands and lower arms are covered with dark paint and black shiny hair hangs over her face as she bends close covering and re-covering the paper. I look at the children with their paint brushes mid air, their eyes on Kiet, and say, "When you were little you got to paint like that, Kiet never got to paint like that so now she's having her turn." They look at me eyes wide, then at Kiet and then at their paintings. Their faces soften. Kiana carefully slides her painting back across the table. She is next to Kiet now. Michael and Marcus slide their paintings along opposite Kiet and Rachael settles back out into her once crammed spot, Georgiy beside her. They dip their brushes into the pots and return to their paintings of pointy roofed houses, yellow suns, green trees with branches and leaves, mums and dads, sisters and brothers—some full bodied with legs and arms, fingers and toes, crooked smiles, eyes, noses, ears, and even hair in pigtails. I smile with them and we chat quietly about their paintings. I walk back to the writing table. "Miss Camden Pratt," a hand tugs at my skirt, "Yes Georgiy?" He looks at me, his eyes big and brown, "Can I have a turn?" I stop, my heart skips a beat, what if I say "yes," what if the principal walks in and they are all painting with their fingers; their hands and arms covered in muddy colors their paintings formless full of movement and tension? "Surely you must have painted like that when you were little Georgiy?" I hold my breath willing him to say "yes." His bottom lip trembles, his eyes grow bigger, rounder. "No, I didn't." I breathe a long deep breath and look at him, his gentle open face, his eyes colored sad. "Yes," I say, "Of course you can." I watch him anxiously and I keep one eye on the classroom door. His fingertips touch the paint onto his paper making spots. His face grimaces. Georgiy goes to the sink and washes his hands, returns to the table and takes up his paintbrush.

In their orderly space of four groups participating in the carefully planned activities of the English literacy curriculum, Kiet has been placed in the group that is painting homes and families. But her reading of this activity is not the same as the others. She has read this space as one in which she may engage in radically different activity from the others in her group. The children literally shrink away from Kiet, not able to imagine, or to constitute themselves as part of a grouping that includes her. She does not heed their horrified withdrawal to the other end of the table, nor the teacher's quiet gaze. She is absorbed in the haecceity of the green and purple paint and the movement of her fingers. While the others engage in the activity the teacher has designed for them that will lead to writing and to representations of themselves in relation to their families, Kiet is caught up in some as yet incomprehensible becoming. The other students are engaged in painting their homes and families and she seems to be engaged in something else, something messy, something inappropriate, something disobedient to the teacher's instructions—and is quite evidently not one of them. Georgiy gently and quietly, and disapprovingly, draws the teacher into their space so she can solve the problem—bring Kiet into line, into the striations of their table and its activity—and so make it safe again. But the teacher does not bring Kiet into line; she sees that Kiet's continuing absorption in her finger painting is not going to allow her to break in; she imagines a soundless waterfall in monsoon rains as she gazes at Kiet and wonders, waits and listens. In waiting the teacher opens up her own line of flight with respect to her planned outcomes for this activity and through doing so creates conditions for the children in Kiet's group to open their own lines of flight into becoming subjects in relation to Kiet's other.

She offers the children (and Kiet if she is listening) a way to give permission to Kiet to continue. The teacher opens the space up to a new idea; they have all done this messy stuff before; they have had their turn; and Kiet must now be given the space to do it too—a simple matter of taking turns. It need not count as a disruption. They do not need to cast her out; she can be in their group and be different. Their membership of a group that is engaged in painting their families and houses, the trees and shining suns is not compromised by Kiet's difference. In chatting to the children about what they are doing she affirms that their interpretation of their task also makes sense. Her choice of the term "turn-taking" could be read as putting Kiet in the category of one who is disadvantaged, or behind the other children in development—"different." And it could be read, in a Deleuzian sense of differenciation, as affirming Kiet in her line of flight, engaging in her own as yet incomprehensible process of becoming, without knowing where it is headed or what risks are involved. The other children seem to read the idea of turns as no more than an affirmation of what they are doing, and as permission for Kiet to do something else while still being a member of the group. The teacher makes Kiet recognizable to them, as being like them, even in her difference. They can imagine what it is like to move the paint around with their fingers because they have done it, too. And they realize it's OK to paint like this if you have not had your chance to do it before, even if you are a student in big school.

What the teacher accomplishes here is a shifting of the ground of what will count as "different" and "other" and who will be counted as someone to be moved away from. Kiet is seen at first by the children as different in a difficult way and as "other"—but the teacher draws their attention to the fact that what she is doing is familiar. What the teacher's words accomplish is a shift in the terms of recognition; Kiet is the same as you; she is just having a turn of something you have had a turn of in the past. Kiet's differenciation was once theirs. But Georgiy can still only see Kiet as "other" and "different" since it seems he too missed out on finger-painting. He has a dilemma. He is part of a community into which Kiet has been accepted on this new ground of shared activity. He does not know how to recognize Kiet in her difference. He must become like her, and paint with his fingers. His desire, where "desire is that which generates life; enabling bodily connections, and social relations" (Hickey-Moody and Malins, 2007: 14), is to bridge the gap that has opened up between himself and the others, himself and Kiet. This in turn generates conflict for the teacher—if this becomes what everyone wants, her classroom might lose its capacity to resemble what the principal expects to see when she walks in. She might no longer be recognizable as a good teacher. Can she risk opening her classroom to more than one child who is different, whose line of flight goes outside the molar lines? Her willingness to take the risk of becoming unrecognizable to her principal, enables Georgiy to resolve his dilemma about being, now, the only one who has never painted with his fingers. He uses the striated concept of "turns" to gain access to Kiet's line of flight. He takes a risk, moving beyond the already-known, and into a dangerous but necessary place. He takes his line of flight into potential chaos. The teacher anxiously watches the door aware of possible consequences of her opening of the lines of flight for the children. But Georgiy concludes his experiment and rapidly folds himself back into the orderly space of the designated activity, now able both to include Kiet in her difference, and to be included in this small community around the table.

Ceppi and Zini write about "a context of overall softness" capable of providing individuals with "spaces for privacy and pause" while still being part of a group (1998: 3). Kiet took up this space alongside her fellow learners; she was simultaneously private and in her own world while being held in community. This was facilitated by the teacher's strategy of attention, which enabled her to recognize Kiet's difference without according her "other" status. To do this she must de-territorialize the school's molar lines of force, and step outside the space that has been "constructed according to a formal framework and a functional order" (Ceppi and Zini, 1998: 2). This requires willingness and a capacity to listen to the student's learning processes which sit outside the designated outcomes of the functional order. It is a political act in which the teacher makes the choice for student process and listens to student voice. In this listening the teacher listens out and in: out to the children, out/in to her professional knowledge as teacher and into herself as a woman once a child.

The teacher's responses are ones formed in relationality, which include her background knowledge of child development, the skills required for literacy and her critical awareness of available pedagogies. She is well aware of the outcomes-based curricula in which she is working and knows that Kiet is not performing like a Kindergarten child but rather like a much younger child in an early childhood setting. On a deeper more personal level the teacher recognizes the trance-like state of Kiet's art making as akin to those states the teacher had entered though drawing in a therapeutic context. Her personal therapeutic work in the years prior to her teaching Kiet also allowed her to respect the process in which Kiet was engaged without needing to know its contents. This allowed the teacher to make sense of Kiet's art making both within and beyond educational development discourses. Her challenge was its place in the classroom context.

Part 2
Kiet painted this way for two terms. Always the same movements, always the repetition, always the colors merging into dynamic mud and always the private world she entered. Painting after painting; sometimes one in a morning, sometimes two, three or more. At times she

packed them up wet layer on wet layer in little parcels for me "For your boys Miss CCP," her crooked teeth in a big smile, her forehead eased out. One morning at the end of the second term in the week I was writing half yearly reports, Kiet drew herself for the first time; full bodied with fingers and toes, full faced with a smile, eyes, a nose and hair, and with the sun in the sky. She wrote her name for the first time, large shaky letters with a capital K. Kiana, Georgiy and Rachael ran across the room to tell me with wide eyes, big smiles and excited voices, "Miss CCP—come and see what Kiet's done—she's written her name." Kiet smiled at me, "See Miss CCP, sunny sun's shining." All twenty-four of us clapped and cheered Kiet; "Miss CCP can we take Kiet up the Primary and show them what she's done?" It took until almost Playtime for Kiet, Kiana, Georgiy and Rachael to get back. I re-wrote Kiet's school report—ticking the outcome indicator of "is able to write her own name without support."

The joy of the community of children in Kiet's achievement is deeply moving. They have enfolded her, safely during all these weeks and months, not knowing where she is headed—or if she is even headed anywhere—recognizing her in her sameness (we too have painted with our fingers) and difference (we now paint with brushes and write our names). They create community with each other, and with the teacher, which embodies Ceppi's and Zini's ideas on community:

> Community in the sense of empathy, a closeness that creates bonds, that enables each group member to recognize the other and to recognize him/herself in the other...Community as the internalization of the other as a value, enabling the construction of common values and shared meanings... Community is a form and a quality of space that fosters encounters, exchange, empathy and reciprocity. (Ceppi and Zini, 1998: n.p.)

The teacher's careful listening, her strategy of attention, her capacity to recognize Kiet and to show the children how to do the same, creates a situation in which their joy bursts forth in applause and pride when Kiet becomes recognizable in the ways they have been unfolding for themselves in the space of the kindergarten classroom. They eagerly extend the recognition of her achievement beyond the walls of the classroom, into the broader school community, asking bigger children and their teachers to become part of the community who recognizes Kiet as one of them.

The teacher de-territorializes the school's molar lines of force and opens herself to potentially dangerous lines of flight as she steps outside the formal framework of the Kindergarten space for a period of two terms. During these two terms the teacher works with Kiet in a variety of ways. Aside from ongoing curriculum support in each Key Learning Area, she assists her in finding words to name and express her feelings. The teacher does this when Kiet is calm and happy working/playing with her classmates as well as when she is troubled and angry with them. She also finds ways to build on Kiet's compassion for her classmates through having her assist others when they are upset or needing help. The teacher also builds a strong and mutually supportive relationship with Kiet's parents so they work closely together to facilitate Kiet's positive engagement in kindergarten. The teacher's interventions with Kiet are grounded in building understandings of difference *and* differenciation within the community of learners in the classroom through story, literature, music and play activities. As it turned out, Kiet's activity eventually takes up the same striations as the others; she takes up the education practices the teacher has designed for her. She re-enters "the fold." She is safely enfolded, shepherded, at one with the others, contained. Not because she was compelled, not because the pedagogical space required it, but because she could explore the intensities and flows of the finger painting when these were what compelled her, and then open herself up to the same intensities and flows as the others, delighting in the act of writing and representation; "See Miss CCP, sunny sun's shining." She has generated intensities in paint, experiencing and experimenting with her own private haecceity, her own acts of becoming, of differenciation, within the safe place of the kindergarten, a space in which she was not abjected and where she was not categorized as other or strange. Her line of flight has taken her to the place that enables her to take up, within the embrace of her community, the skills and capacities that the teacher has in mind for her and enable her to achieve the outcomes desired for a Kindergarten child.

Returning to art making and relationality

Kiet used art to accomplish something, to express something that is at the time she begins kindergarten, inexpressible. She works over a long period of time, almost half a year, before the work she is engaged in is done. Her intense involvement in her art creates dilemmas for her teacher. Artistic work, artistic-becoming, is not necessarily joyful and pleasurable, and easy to recognize and to support—though it may be that. It seems that Kiet's art making is pleasurable for her and it simultaneously challenges the teacher as to how she can best support Kiet's becoming. In a Deleuzian sense, artistic becoming may hold elements of seeming madness; that is, it necessitates working in ways that may not be comprehensible to either the artist or the observer. Such art is not compatible with neoliberal end-product models of education where standard accomplishments can be ticked off inside orderly, imposed time frames. Art such as Kiet's is more understandable as process rather than product. As Springgay says in relation to her own art classroom, art working is a complex sentient form of inquiry, where inner being and bodily materiality are in relation to, enmeshed with, outside materiality. Inner and outer cannot be separated in the movement that is opened up through the art work. The artist is engaged in becoming in the same movement as the creation of the art work. The artist is, in this sense, vulnerable to change and to transformation:

> This transformation cannot happen unless we embrace the vulnerability of inquiry. Vulnerability recognizes that knowledge is felt, that it is sentient, embodied, and deep. Rather than a view that understands interior knowledge as inferior, intercorporeality un/folds inside and outside disrupting patterns in an attempt to create meaning through entanglements and spatial re-alignments—a mapping as trace and as process. (Springgay, 2008: 94-5)

For teachers curriculum guidelines and national standards may not be useful documents to guide or even comprehend this vulnerability and opening up to the new. This may mean that teachers are often required to navigate without a map, without guidelines that provide a clear path to be followed. This means that teacher vulnerability may well be present at the same time as student vulnerability. The teacher's relationship with her vulnerability is crucial then in the kinds of spaces she can open up for artistic becoming in classrooms.

In this story teacher vulnerability is present alongside student vulnerability. bell hooks suggests teacher vulnerability is crucial in what she calls engaged pedagogy: "Engaged pedagogy does not seek simply to empower students. Any classroom that employs a holistic model of learning will also be a place where teachers grow, and are empowered by the process. This empowerment cannot happen if we refuse to be vulnerable while encouraging students to take risks" (hooks, 1994: 21). The teacher's vulnerability although not the same as Kiet's nevertheless lies alongside Kiet's as she supports her in an art making process that the teacher herself does not know for certain will lead to the curriculum outcomes. The teacher sits with her teacher vulnerability and opens into the space it offers. There the teacher finds a way through drawing on her professional and personal knowledge. While the teacher's vulnerability as she allows Georgiy to explore painting with his fingers is quickly resolved as he returns to the more orderly painting task, it enables her to explore her own line of flight with regard to classroom management and her performance of herself as a teacher. In this way it prepares her for how to address possible questioning of her professionalism by her school principal. Teacher vulnerability then becomes a resource to be opened up, something to be worked with, rather than an experience to be dismissed, shut down or foreclosed. It becomes a strength in a pedagogical encounter.

The teacher and students constitute together a relationality in which vulnerability can be held, so that lines of flight using art making in the art of becoming, are possible. Relationality lies at the heart of the philosophy of pedagogy and space that we are seeking to develop in this book. It unsettles ideas of the singular, autonomous subject whose life is somehow conceived outside relations with the other. It moves toward a conception of plural being, of being-with-one-another and addressing-one-another (Nancy, 2000). In this story, Kiet seeks relationality beyond the classroom and into the teacher's life by giving her paintings as "gifts" to the teacher's children. It is evident through this act that not only is Kiet seeking a wider relationality, it may also indicate the value she herself places on her self and her art making—she is worthy of inclusion in the teacher's family and her painting is something of worth, something given as a gift.

The pedagogical space in the story is a relational space with a focus on listening, and on strategies of attention; it is defined by openness and softness, and also by the management of conflicts and contradictions lying at its heart. Here art making as pedagogy is about movement, about folding and unfolding, about openness to difference and to change. In this there must be openness and a strategy of attention to the many small moments of de-individualization, in which both teachers and students escape "the limits of the individual" (Roffe, 2007: 43). These small escapes, these lines of flight, these slides toward the not-yet-known, are moments of *becoming,* in which there is also a "constitution of new ways of being in the world, new ways of thinking and feeling, new ways of being a subject" (Roffe, 2007: 43). Working together as teachers and students in the not-yet-known facilitates teacher and student capacity to be altered through this engagement with self and Other. In the story this working together takes place in a subtle and material space which requires as well as enables a paradoxically safe vulnerability.

Todd observes that it is this not-yet-known that lies at the heart of relationality in educational contexts: "our commitment to our students involves our capacity to be altered, to become someone different than we were before; and, likewise, our students' commitment to social causes through their interactions with actual people equally consists in their capacity to be receptive to the Other to the point of transformation" (Todd, 2003: 89). Art making allows entry into and expression of the not-yet-known. In the educational context, art making opens students and teacher to opportunities for transformation.

In this story these new ways of being, thinking, feeling and of being a subject are enabled through art making in community. Here we cannot directly see or indeed interpret the influence of art making *in* community on Kiet. However, it is evident that for the children engaged in art making with her there is a direct influence. I suggest that the relational space in which the art making took place and which the art making in turn influenced, gave Kiet a secure communally creative space which all the children inhabited together as they worked. While existentially alone as she entered the chaotic world that the art making space opened up for her, Kiet worked alongside her full-bodied classmates within a noisy hum of children's voices just like her own. Art making gave her an opportunity to focus on listening to herself, to activate her strategies of attention; it allowed her to be open and soft in order to manage the conflicts and contradictions lying at the heart of her interior and exterior relational spaces. It was a safe place that could hold her chaotic inner world as she made and re-made art in the service of her be-coming.

Kiet and the other children, and the teacher, are engaged in a form of relationality that, in Ceppi's and Zini's terms, is characterized by "an openness and attention to others as a value, respect for differences, however they may be expressed: differences of race, religion, sex and culture, [and] extending more generally to any kind of diversity" (1998: 2). Each child is thus engaged in his or her differentiation and elaboration at the molecular level, adapting and developing their own capacities to engage with others. To support this work: "The school environment must be flexible over time and *manipulatable*. It must also change and be open to *modification* by the children's processes of *self-learning* and, in turn, interact with those processes and modify them" (Ceppi and Zini, 1998: 11).

This second part of Kiet's story shows how "it is the learning individual (herself) who, by interacting with reality, constructs and deconstructs reality, makes transformations, creates reticular connections among the elements of the learning that is taking place" (Ceppi and Zini, 1998: 10). The teacher trusted both Kiet and Georgiy in their engagement with self-learning, in their *becoming*. Each communicated, in their different ways, the potentially transformative point they had arrived at, a point that enabled them to work with sameness and difference, through repetition and movement. The molar and constraining lines of force are embodied in the principal and lived out through the contemporary educational discourse dominated by an "overriding concern for instrumentality, effectiveness, skills, competencies, standardization, and other means of leveling nuance and banishing irreconcilables" (Roy, 2004: 297). These must give way to the thisness of the moment for such learning to take place. As Albrecht-Crane and Slack observe:

> What happens in the classroom, its 'thisness', often exceeds what is perceived as the task at hand and engulfs students and teachers in spaces of 'affect' in ways that matter in the politics of everyday life. This is not just a space of learning but a political space where social beings interact with implications in larger political and cultural struggles. The classroom is where life takes place and where politics happens, even—perhaps especially—in moments that are seemingly insignificant or mundane. Teachers and students are often caught up in encounters that conjure affective 'sense-ations'—moments of energetic and resonant connection—which indicate that something significant is at work. (Albrecht-Crane and Slack, 2007: 99)

Art making opens up spaces and opportunities for "thisness" and enables the art of becoming. Student becoming is political. The influence of teacher agency in student becoming is evident in this story. Creating conditions in which students and teachers are able to take lines of flight becomes a political act with implications for the individual and the community. The story in this chapter raises questions of teacher responsibility in creating classroom conditions which enable all the children to take their lines of flight, and her role in co-creating with them a community in which this is possible. Yet the tensions implicit in this responsibility are evident in the story and its discussion and the creation of such an environment is in doubt given the increasing pressures of rigid schooling systems. How teachers support each other in engaging with students in differenciation becomes itself political, becomes part of the art of teacher becoming.

As I finish this chapter the noisy colorful hum of the Kindergarten room fades and I think about how just a few weekends ago I sat around a table with Kiana and Kiet, having lunch with them and their mothers. They are no longer children—they are now young women not long out of High School and making plans for their futures. Kiana is taller than me. They are both beautiful, confident young women excited by the uncertainties of life beyond school. As we reminisce and share stories of our year together all those years ago I marvel at the layers of our relationships. They ask lots of questions about how come I taught them the way I did and are eager to know what lay behind my classroom practices. I talk with them about art making and learning in and through community and how each child in their class contributed to the progress made by all the children. They remind me of things I said and did, of what they and other children said and did, and in amongst the laughter we talk about Kiet's challenges and what they meant for her and the class community. She sits across from me, with her once crooked teeth straightened into a warm big smile, her black stylish haircut framing her open face. Kiet only vaguely remembers giving me her paintings for my sons, but both remember clearly how they visited each classroom the day Kiet wrote her name, proudly showing Kiet's drawing with her name in big shaky letters. We talk about the metaphor of sunny sun and the stories I told them about the sun's adventures, hiding behind clouds while she waited for the rain to fall, and how she was always shining somewhere in the world even when it was night-time in our sky. I am struck by their maturity and Kiet's insight into her life challenges. I am privileged to have stayed in touch with Kiet and her family over the years. As a result of a lot of hard work, she has successfully completed her Higher School Certificate. After many years of searching, her parents recently found and established contact with her birth mother, who, in a few weeks time, Kiet will meet for the first time in her life.

And so...

In this chapter I have explored the idea of art making and becoming through the story of a child's line of flight and its consequences for herself, her fellow classmates and her teacher in a state-run kindergarten.

I have begun to flesh out the art of becoming that teachers and their students engage in, in the space of classrooms, where relationality and community are centered. It has raised the tensions that exist for individual teachers who set out to enable and support individual lines of flight. In the context of the current outcomes-driven curriculum, it is possible for teachers to have agency, and to find ways to facilitate the individual and collective arts of becoming.

In the next chapter Susanne works again with attention to difference and to the possibilities that enable teachers to open up the possibilities of differenciation both for themselves and their students. Drawing on her memories of being an English teacher with Aboriginal students and foreign exchange students in two quite different contexts, she explores the possibilities and constraints of secondary schools. She focuses in particular on cultural difference, and develops the concept and practice of ethical encounter. She extends her analyses from classrooms into the broader national context as she considers the "Sorry" speech of the Australian Prime Minister as a pedagogical encounter.

Notes

Thank you to Bronwyn Davies for her detailed contributions to the analysis of Kiet's story.

[i] In the class of twenty-four children there were a number of children who experienced significant life challenges.

4
DIFFERENCE AS ETHICAL ENCOUNTER
SUSANNE GANNON

This chapter works further into the notion of "difference" in pedagogical encounters by exploring two collective biography stories alongside a third text, an excerpt from the Australian Prime Minister's historic 2008 speech on the stolen generations. I argue that this speech can also be read as a pedagogical encounter with its own particular spatial, temporal and affective modalities and performances. Each of these texts draws attention to an ethics of encounter and responsibility and to notions of difference within pedagogical space.

While one of the collective biography stories focuses on a young white teacher in a class of Aboriginal children, the other story traces the same teacher's experience some years later with international exchange students. Both of these stories are provocations to investigate ethical relations between pedagogies, bodies and space, but in their sense-making they invoke differences of skin, language, belief, taste and culture, class and privilege, or lack of it, that appear to separate the teacher and her students, and to separate students from each other. These binaries of self/other and the language of diversity and inclusion/exclusion invoke categorical differences rather than the more radical Deleuzian process of differenciation through which differences are continuously decomposing, reproducing and multiplying and where "the subject itself is the locus of effects of his or her surroundings" (Bell, 2007: 11). This chapter draws attention to the subject of the teacher, to the particular teacher who is evoked in the situations and surroundings described in these stories and who haunts me again, many years later, as I sit here one summer morning in Sydney writing this chapter.

The theoretical risks in this chapter include reinstating a stable humanist self who is engaged in a project of personal/professional/ intellectual self development. Rather I attempt to focus on the specificities of each embodied and spatially and temporally situated pedagogical encounter—on the subject as the "locus of effects of her surroundings"—without assuming continuity between the teacher subject across the particular classrooms. Nor do I claim autonomy for the subject who takes herself up as the teacher in these sites. Like the other classrooms described in this book, the secondary English classrooms in the stories are regulating and regulated spaces within which teacher and students engage in particular pedagogical performances constrained by curriculum, timetables, resources, furniture, architecture and elaborate hierarchies of authority. Yet I argue through my analyses that the pedagogical encounters within them are "determined but not fully determined" allowing for meetings which involve both "surprise and conflict" (Ahmed, 2000: 6). In Ahmed's interpretation of the embodied encounter "identity is instituted through encounters with others that surprise, that shift the boundaries of the familiar, of what we assume that we know" (2000: 7). Much contemporary schooling is contingent on reinforcing the notion of the teacher as she who "knows" (as classroom manager, curriculum implementer, sociologist, even adolescent psychologist) and of students as knowable. The teacher in the classrooms in this chapter is caught out in her unknowing, she is surprised and in some ways undone as she endeavors to engage with her students and to engage her students in learning. In these pedagogical encounters between particular bodies in time and space, lines of flight open up the art of becoming.

Another risk in this chapter entails overlooking the social injustices that have ensued from categorical differences. Here I wish to destabilize categories of difference, whilst maintaining awareness of how they work in the world.

The representation of the students in the opening paragraph of this chapter as "Aboriginal" and as "international exchange students" and of the teacher as "white" is already indicative of the inclination to stratification in much contemporary education as well as broader understandings of the social. Although in a Deleuzian sense bodies are in a state of continuous change, they are socially regulated and "stratified" because they are "arranged within grid-like categories such as sex, gender, color, ethnicity, religion, sexuality, age and ability" (Hickey-Moody and Malins, 2007: 5). Discourses of equity and diversity demand the simultaneous recognition and erasure of students through grids of identity which often operate to constrain flows, and limit connections and potentialities. In the stories told in this chapter "identity" is tethered, at least partially and through the perspective of the teacher, to notions of ethnic and racial difference. In contrast, in a Deleuzian reading, difference is seen as multiple and distributed across classrooms in heterogeneous and constantly shifting configurations. Although difference is dispersed it "coagulates" in particular subjects who are embedded and invested in particular sorts of identities.[i] Nevertheless, as some of the discussion in this chapter shows, it can be mobilized for specific purposes at particular times and in particular places.

Each of the three texts is particularly concerned with racial difference, which, although it can be understood as a deeply unstable social construct, has marked material effects in the world. Grosz reminds us that "the various distinctions and categories that mark race today are historically variable, politically motivated, and highly volatile in their operations; but it is also clear that there are systematic, visible differences between groups of individuals that we can mark in various, perhaps arbitrary ways" (2008b: 47-48). Consequently, although "race itself may be based on error, the effects of race or race 'politics' most certainly exist" (Lampert, 2009: 31). In addition, race in Australia, and in different parts of Australia, has particular contours that differ from those that mark racial "categories" elsewhere. The stories in this chapter demonstrate how "race"—whether it is Aboriginal, Japanese, Chilean and/or Anglo-Australian—is associated with differences of language, knowledge, gestures, bodily practices, and degrees of privilege and disadvantage. The Prime Minister's speech further articulates how practices of racialization were institutionalized by government, and how the nation itself has been predicated on racial binaries. In her most recent work, which makes comprehensive use of Deleuze, Bell argues that rather than eliminating or ignoring such categories, it is incumbent upon us to recognize the "tenacity" of group identities and to admit into our theorizing the "felt modalities of the temporal" (Bell, 2007: 32). My discussion of the pedagogical encounters in this chapter aims to explore these felt modalities, from the particular positions of the white Anglo-Australian subject who is teacher, student and, most recently, audience to the Prime Minister's speech of apology.

Difference in Deleuze and Levinas

The discussion in this chapter ventures into the highly charged political space and time of reconciliation politics in Australia and it is for that reason that I have found it productive to bring work influenced by philosopher Emmanuel Levinas (Ahmed, 2000; Bell, 1996, 2007; Diprose, 2001; Todd, 2003) to the Deleuzian theoretical assemblage in order to complicate understandings of what is ethically and educationally at stake in theorizing difference. This is not an easy alliance but rather an opportunity to think through some of the spaces between the work of Levinas and Deleuze. Although both are generally understood as poststructural philosophers working within a particular historical, social and intellectual milieu, and although they were contemporaries, dying in France just six weeks apart in 1995, their work is not often thought together. However Bell (1996, 2006, 2007) and May (1997) have been two theorists who have done this work. May argues that, along with Nancy and Derrida, the work of Levinas and Deleuze converged on the problem of "how to conceive difference and how to valorize it" (1997: 2). He argues that Deleuze and Levinas both understood "difference as a constitutive element in some part of our experience" and that in their theoretical work they both privileged "difference over identity" (May, 1997: 3). They rejected the familiar sociological accounts of identity which tend to "make static the complexity and contingency of what we might term...the narrativisation of identity" (Bell, 1996: 224). In Deleuzian terms, racialization can be understood as "a process involving lines of light and of enunciation, of power and subjectification, that entwine in the placing of people within racial categories" (Bell, 1996: 221). Elsewhere she describes the effects of these "lines of light and enunciation" as ensuring that, in the operations of power and violence, "what is readable on the body is only ever the embodiment, momentary if seamlessly reiterated, of forces that emanate from without" (Bell, 2006: 215) She argues that identity categories and positions, including that of "race," are experienced at varying "depths." Although such categories are inherently performative and thus neither essential nor inevitable, Bell argues that feminist and poststructural accounts need to better acknowledge "the *sense* of identity, its *felt* embodiment, and the inextricability and undesirability of removing one's attachment to identity" (2007: 32). She finds the notion of "chaining" in Levinas' work particularly helpful for theorizing "embodied relations to the past" in the form of attachments to historically and socially constituted identity categories (2007: 33). Although chaining is "genealogically conferred and embodied" it is also a *practice* and therefore it is "contingent, contextualized, intermittent and temporal" (Bell, 2007: 36). The collective biography stories in this chapter, along with the Prime Minister's speech, trace how these iterative attachments, or "chainings," manifest and reverberate amongst individuals and institutions and begin to draw attention to their profound material effects.

Difference as Ethical Encounter

The Deleuzian notion of "stratification" can also be used to account for the tenacity of identity. Common discourses of diversity in education tend to instantiate and reinscribe identity categories in order to provide grounds for discussion of equity issues. In contrast, in the continuous internal process of differenciation, according to Deleuze, difference is "never a negation but a creation, and difference is never negative but essentially positive and creative" (Deleuze, 1988: 94, cited in Bell, 2007: 106). The process of individuation by which we become recognizable to ourselves and others is "mobile, strangely supple, fortuitous and endowed with fringes and margins; all because the intensities which contribute to it communicate with each other, envelop other intensities and are in turn enveloped" (Deleuze, 1994: 257). The teacher and students who are discussed in this chapter are initially made comprehensible in terms of their locations on particular grids of identity, but they are also engaged in destabilizing the grid in embodied moments of connection. In particular moments in the stories, the teacher is caught beginning to think and move and feel differently in relation to and with her students. She might be understood to be following the advice of Deleuze and Guattari:

> [F]irst see how [the social formation] is stratified for us and in us and at the place where we are; then descend from the strata to the deeper assemblage within which we are held; gently tip the assemblage...to reveal connection of desires, conjunction of flows, continuum of intensities. (Deleuze and Guattari, 1987: 161)

The Prime Minister's story, too, the pedagogical encounter of the national speech, mobilizes affect in such a way that new connections and conjunctions between bodies become possible. There is a momentary "drift" away from the grid—from striated space into smooth space, to new becomings, and therefore to new potential futures.

Affect is central and this understanding of pedagogical encounters emphasizes the possibilities of dissolution of affective subjects in encounter rather than their solidification. "Becoming," in Braidotti's readings of Deleuze, is "to do with emptying out the self, opening it to possible encounters with the 'outside'" (2006: 145). Such an encounter is a "relational bond that simultaneously propels the self out of the black hole of its atomized isolation and disperses it into a myriad of bits and pieces," that also "confirms the singularity of that particular entity which both receives and recomposes itself around the onrush of data and affects" (Braidotti, 2006: 145). Affect is crucial in mobilizing response in pedagogical encounters. Thinking through affect brings the sensory capacity of the body to the fore. Affect is visceral. It precedes the articulations of language and thought. It is felt in the body before it is overladen with meaning. The children and the teacher in each pedagogical encounter—each of them learning and teaching from one another in new ways in every instant—and the Prime Minister in his pedagogical encounter with the nation—are brought into an affective and ethical relationality marked by what Levinas might call "a carnal generosity" (Diprose, 2001: 14). This generosity is not premised on the preservation of a discrete and separate self nor on the operations of an agentic rational will emanating from any individual, but it is an embodied affective and ethical demand that arises from "a being-put-into-question that makes me responsible for the other that moves me" (Diprose, 2001: 125). Levinas, like Deleuze, favors a subjectivity premised on movement and relationality, but the ethical encounters he theorizes are sensitive to socio-historical contexts and materiality—and they are contingent on a vulnerability to the other in any embodied encounter. As Diprose says, it is "the body engaged in projects that expresses meaning as it assembles being, with reference not to a pre-cultural reality but to the historical and cultural context in which it is located" (2001: 128). Bell argues that to focus on subject or object, or on the "the nature of difference" is inadequate, rather she suggests that "one must follow the curves to reveal the constitutive forces that animate the scene, that constitute the object and its contemporary intelligibility" (2007: 101). In a Deleuzian paradigm we might understand collective biography as a methodology that invites investigations of "the body engaged in projects" in Diprose's terms, or where we "follow the curves...that animate a scene" in Bell's terms. Bringing in Levinas, through Bell, Diprose and Ahmed enables consideration of an ethics of responsibility materialized in pedagogical encounters.

Give him your alien kindness

The first story describes the strange encounters of two foreign exchange students in an Australian high school in the late 1990s. This experienced teacher's professional identity is tied up with her sense of what she knows about teaching, and how she embodies herself as a teacher. The story here works its way gradually towards an explicit and particular encounter—a poetry reading—during which the whole class was affected, and brought into an ethical relation that took them by surprise and opened new possibilities for being in the world.

She had two exchange students in her small 'year eleven' English class, Diego and Hiro. Diego from Chile had already finished his schooling and was spending the year here before he went home to university. Japanese Hiro was small and quiet and young and had a difficult time with his host families and from the other kids until they found that he was good at soccer. One morning she brought a box of takeaway sushi to school, an extra box she'd bought for him as an afterthought the night before. When she gave it to him, he cried. She wanted to hug him, but she couldn't so she patted his arm ineffectually and murmured as he struggled to keep the tears from spilling down his face.

Later in the year, in English, the students had been looking at dramatic monologue with her and reading the poetry of contemporary Australian poet Bruce Dawe. For Weapons Training she had lined up volunteers at the front of the class, transformed her gait and her voice and became a major swaggering up and down the line, eyeballing different 'soldiers' and barking the lines of the poem: "grab and check the magazine man, it isn't a woman's tit" and "you know what you are? You're dead dead dead." She meant to shock them with the performative potential of language. They talked about the context and era of the poem and of what Dawe might have been trying to achieve. They talked about how else one might perform this poem to bring out all the nuances of meaning. They talked about tone and projection and body language, props and costumes. Then it was the students' turn. They could work individually or in pairs, choose their own Dawe poem and perform it in any way they liked for the rest of the class. They had a few lessons to plan and rehearse and then a day was set aside for performances. She would help anyone who asked but was just as willing to be surprised by their inventiveness.

On the day, Jacob did his poem about consumer culture and voyeurism from inside a cardboard television set that sat on his shoulders. Then Diego and Hiro stood up. They had chosen Dawe's Advice to an interplanetary visitor, a poem that sketched a post-apocalyptic earth visited by aliens who find the last lonely human. It finishes with "when you find him— / give him your alien kindness, / stroke him with feelers of love." They performed a choral reading, line by line, drawing out the sadness and the beauty of the poem with their pace. Diego said the first line in Spanish, then Hiro said it in Japanese in the same solemn tone, an *utterly strange echo, carrying all they knew of homesickness and the depth of their displacement out to us, sitting silent at the classroom desks.*

Like the teacher, the other students were immersed in the impossible strangeness of language, feeling for just these six minutes what these two had been feeling for the whole year. Her eyes prickled and she struggled to stop herself from crying. They finished, paused, looked up at us in the desks, and the whole class burst into clapping and hooping and foot stomping. They had shifted something for all of us. And of course she gave them both A+.

The story pivots on two moments of crying, or of struggling not to cry. Both the boy and the teacher are brought into an affective space, a space of radical vulnerability to the other. In the first instance the teacher's actions provoke tears in Hiro, while in the second instance, it is Hiro and Diego who bring the teacher to the edge of tears. The teacher comes to "know" the students for an instant in a different way. Initially the teacher mentions that, as an "afterthought," she bought an extra box of sushi and brought it to school for the homesick boy from Japan. Although sushi takeaway has become the most clichéd symbol of Japanese influence in Australia, the gesture is nevertheless moving for the boy: it moves him to tears. In her work on postcolonial bodies, Ahmed emphasizes that "strange bodies are produced through tactile encounters with other bodies" and that it is "the very acts and gestures whereby subjects differentiate between others that constitute the permeability of social and bodily space" (2000: 15). Social space has been permeated and the teacher is becoming-other in this moment when "a body connects to another body and...begins to move, think and feel in new ways" (Hickey-Moody and Malins, 2007: 6). The gift of the day-old sushi does not overcome the political and social differences between teacher and student. The teacher still cannot comprehend the scale of the homesickness experienced by the student. They are separated further by gender and age as the older woman watches the young man try not to behave in an unmanly way. What the teacher learns from this encounter is the breadth of the gap between them. She says she wants to hug him but can't—at this late stage in her career she is well aware of directives on professional behavior and child safety—so she pats his arm ineffectually and murmurs. Though there are limitations to their touching, she too is touched, she is "moved from her place" (Ahmed, 2000: 40).

The poetry reading takes place several months later. The exchange students have had some time to come "home" in this place that is theirs for the year. Hiro has moved from an unsatisfactory host family to the home of another teacher and is now more often to be seen smiling at school. The teacher does not feel the need to bring him Japanese food any more. The teacher and class have become used to the foreign visitors and they have become used to the school and the town where the school is located. By now, the boys have had sufficient lived experience of this place that it "intrudes into [their] senses: it defines what one smells, hears, touches, feels, remembers" (Ahmed, 2000: 89). By now, they have begun to experience what Ahmed describes as the leakage of "subject and space" into one another (Ahmed, 2000: 89). Yet, it is just at this point that Hiro and Diego join forces and take up a performative stance that emphasizes their otherness to this place. They become quite literally aliens again, just as teacher and students had become used to them as members of the quasi-community of the class. Although Bruce Dawe, the Australian poet studied in the English class, writes about various types of alienation, together they have chosen the one poem in his oeuvre that is about aliens. Together they become "interplanetary visitors," as they have been to some degree all year. They take up this position by rewriting the poem "Advice to an interplanetary visitor" (Dawe, 2006) into Spanish and Japanese and delivering it, line by oddly echoed line, in languages that make their listeners take a position outside language. As meaning falls away, apart from what is already known of the poem from previous study, the listeners are forced instead to abandon sense and to attend to the displacement—and the alienation—that the language submits them to. They are forced to listen beyond sense. It is in this excessive moment that the teacher feels her eyes prickling and has the same struggle against tears that she detected in Hiro several months earlier. The students' performance entails great generosity and trust. They take a risk in interpreting an English class as a space where they might abandon English. They trust that the teacher and other students will enter the space of vulnerability that they have opened. Their alienation is a sort of gift of who they are, beyond their soccer playing adolescent selves. Most of all, they anticipate that the listeners will be able to listen as they need them to. Todd suggests that listening is at the centre of ethical encounters and entails "a trust that is born of the uncertainty of the communication...where the vicissitudes of language yield unpredictable and unqualifiable narratives" (2003: 125).

This encounter carries a glimpse of what an ethical encounter might look like, what it might entail to open into becoming otherwise. In that moment the classroom appears to have elements of Ceppi's and Zini's classroom as "community" which is characterized by "willingness to listen and be open to others...respect for differences, however they may be expressed...[and a] sense of empathy, a closeness that creates bonds, that enables each group member to recognize the other and to recognize him/herself in the other" (1998: n.p.). However this analysis risks presenting the classroom as a utopian space where students can "express" themselves and become "who they really are," This is the humanist progressivist fantasy of pedagogical space. Although there is mo(ve)ment (Davies and Gannon, 2006) within and among the subjects in the class, the performance of alienation keeps the teacher and class dislocated in language. In their performance of "Advice to an interplanetary visitor," they have found a means of holding together the "proximity and distance" that Ahmed argues, after Levinas, are crucial for ethical communication (2000: 157). Yet this account of the event—from the teacher's perspective—has revealed some of the "connection of desires, conjunction of flows, continuum of intensities" (Deleuze and Guattari, 1987: 161) that arise in (this) pedagogical place.

Although there is some sense of reciprocal touching, of an affective ripple through the classroom from students to the teacher and to other students, and although the possibility for ethical encounters is evident, the classroom is not an equal space. The teacher has orchestrated the conditions of these encounters. Ahmed and Todd both suggest that an element of surprise and unpredictability is necessary for ethical encounters. Part of the work of the teacher is in establishing her classroom as a space that oscillates between smoothness and striations, a space that is both new and replete with possibilities, and tightly controlled. Here it is evident that "some spatial striations are very useful" (Hickey-Moody and Malins, 2007: 11). The teacher has created the conditions for assessment for the poetry performance task that allow a multilingual response and that allow group or individual performance. She has determined that this oral task is to be performed "live" in front of the rest of the class, rather than audio or video taped as some of the other oral tasks throughout the year have been. She has designed the assessment task and the rubric by which it will be assessed, and which she uses to justify the A+ that she awards to the two students. Amongst the criteria that determine an A grade are: "skillfully exploit the potential of a poem in an original interpretation" and "create a strong impact on the audience." In her design of classroom activities the teacher contrives to create conditions within which students can succeed. The students rise to the performance in ways that satisfy the criteria that are detailed on the grid of the assessment rubric, and the response detailed in the story exceeds what had already been demarcated in the grid as "create a strong impact on the audience." The final sentence of the story, with its "of course" and its "A+," reminds us again that in this pedagogical encounter, the smooth space of the new, the moment of transcendence, is also, still, a striated space of institutional conventions that is managed by the teacher.

Wednesday. English. Lesson One

The second memory story in this chapter comes from much earlier in the teacher's career, her first full time job teaching which was in an Aboriginal school in the early 1980s:

Wednesday. English. Lesson One. Five of the kids are out of her class for the first fifteen minutes, as they are every day, getting treated for trachoma by the school nurse. The others are writing at their desks. She can see Brother H at the front of his class at the other end of the long room. He has the Sounds in Color phonics kit out and is using it with his class. Her box stays in the cupboard. She doesn't really have a teacher's desk (she doesn't really feel much like a teacher), but she spends her lesson moving between the desks, talking to the kids, in pairs or individually about what they are writing. They often stroke her white arms while she squats down or sits beside them at their desks talking, or lean against her as they do out in the playground. In the six months since they gave her this class they have already published a small book of stories sent up to the next town to the offset printer because this is before the days of photocopiers and binding machines. They came back in June just in time for the kids to take copies with them in the small planes and Toyotas that cross the desert taking people home for holidays, ceremonies and funerals.

At the beginning of the new term she brought an Australian Geographic magazine in and they worked their way through a long article on bush tucker around Alice Springs. The kids knew the plants in the photos and told her more about them. Some of what was in the article was wrong, or different where they came from. Mary and Frances were in the back corner working on their drawings. With her help they were making a bilingual calendar of drawings and text in both English and Language about the bush tucker in their community: how and when and where to find it and what you had to do to it to get it ready to eat. They were fifteen, women already, and knew everything they needed to know about how to live. Other kids were working on stories about spirits and scary creatures that they knew, like the Red Dress Woman who kidnapped children in certain parts of the town. This project had been started by an Aboriginal teacher and storyteller who had come into their class.

She talked with Peter, a big boy with a grown man's moustache. They both looked down at the page on his desk rather than at each other—at least she knew that much—and slowly his words came out. A start of a story. At last. Before the end of the period. "That's great" she said, "Just scribble that down." He looked at her, lost, "What mean scribble Miss?" How many other words that she used everyday, without even thinking, did he not know? Yet of his languages she knew next to nothing.

At another desk she saw Brian. His book was open, but he was not writing. He was messing about with something else. "What are you doing?" she asked as she walked over. "You should be writing your story." "Can't think Miss," he said. She saw now what he was doing: dropping lice from his hair on to his exercise book and squashing them between his fingernails. The poor kid. How could he think? How could he write? Once again, she wondered—just for a moment though—as she moved closer towards him, if this would be the day she would catch them too.

This teacher says she "doesn't really feel much like a teacher." She isn't a (qualified) teacher, yet, but this experience convinced her that she wanted to be one and she left the school in order to complete a postgraduate teaching degree. At this time, before she knows what she is doing, she rejects the teacher's apparatus as it is represented by the experienced teacher at the other end of the double classroom. That teacher uses a phonics kit but she leaves hers in the cupboard and tries to engage her students with writing tasks that have relevance to what they know. She does not have her students seated in solid rows facing the front but leaves spaces so she can spend the time "moving between the desks, talking to the kids, in pairs or individually about what they are writing." The body of the teacher and the bodies of the students are in proximity throughout the story. These students touch the teacher while she takes on a more passive and receptive mode in relation to their touch: they "often stroke her white arms while she squats down or sits beside them at their desks talking, or lean against her as they do out in the playground."

DIFFERENCE AS ETHICAL ENCOUNTER

Intimacy and difference are produced simultaneously between the subjects in this pedagogical space. The teacher is produced as different by the actions of the students as a "strange body...produced *through tactile encounters with other bodies*: differences are not marked *on* the stranger's body, but come to materialize in the relationship of touch between bodies" (Ahmed, 2000: 15). In the last lines of the story her passive receptivity to her students' bodies is also briefly marked by a passing sense of her own vulnerability where "she wondered—just for a moment—as she moved closer to him, if this would be the day she would catch [lice] too." The teacher moves closer to the boy despite the lice. She is appalled at the conditions that her students suffer while she naively expects them to be able to think or to write. Why does she not think to send him to the school nurse? Perhaps she did but the nurse's attention was predominantly absorbed in trying to stem the chronic disease that would otherwise blind the children. The degree of deprivation astounds her. Though these children live in dormitories with hot water under the supervision of adults she knows that only the girls are provided with shampoo and conditioner. The Commonwealth government funding for the boarders buys an extra pie for the boys from the school canteen each lunchtime.

As well as the social and bodily spaces in the classroom being permeable, so too the pedagogy the teacher is developing emerges from recognizing the permeability of knowledge in and out of schools, and trying to reconfigure what might count as knowledge in school contexts. She has been learning how to learn from the children from an Aboriginal teacher and storyteller, a young woman like herself. The writing that contributes to the book of stories began with storytelling sessions and a range of language enrichment activities designed for her class by this other teacher. The white teacher too knows some things herself that she brings to the classroom. She has, for example, studied Aboriginal Languages at university and has a good theoretical understanding of the syntax, semantics and phonology of these elaborate and complex languages. She knows also that there are considerable differences amongst the students in terms of the languages they know, the country they come from and their kinship obligations. Her other job at the school is helping the Brother who teaches the subject called "Language" in his classes with these children. She brings in *Australian Geographic* because it has an article about bush tucker in the desert, a topic these students have learnt about from birth. She reads the article to and with her students and designs literacy activities from it. When two girls from the desert describe how they harvest and use these plants differently, she has the knowledge to help them write their text in both English and their language. The students' knowledge is recognized as legitimate in the classroom and the teacher becomes a bridge to help the students to express what they know. However she does not know quite how to move them past this. With Peter's "What mean scribble Miss?" she realizes again the gulf between what she knows and what her students need to know and she doesn't know how to bring them fast enough or thoroughly enough to the new knowledges that they will need. Time is short. She recognizes the paradox inherent in trying to teach basic knowledge to these mustachioed young men and these grown young women. The risk that this analysis runs is in romanticizing the intentions and the pedagogical practices that the inexperienced teacher took up in her struggle to engage her students.

Her pedagogy might be seen as a capitulation in the face of the impossibility of teaching these students, so other to her and the middle class white east coast urban Australia she knows. Framing her pedagogy around students' prior knowledge might be seen as an abandonment of the responsibility to teach. For those who advocate compensatory phonics programs for students with poor literacy, her disregard for the Sounds in Color kit might be read as negligent. But in her telling of that moment, in that space, with those bodies and knowledges, she suggests that she does the best she can, and the best or the most ethical way to proceed is to make space and, through an interdisciplinary move, to attempt to legitimize what has not been legitimate school knowledge. These are openings for "lines of flight, knowledge, power and subjectification" (Bell, 2007: 103) that impact in particular on the becoming-teacher. This story hints at an instance of differenciation as an internal process where the teacher brushing up against her students—their skin, language and knowledge—is engaged in becoming different, evolving beyond what she could be or could have known before she was here in this intense and embodied pedagogical space. The students open intensities in her, incite flows between that allow her to become different from who she had been.

The teacher subject in this room is the "locus of effects" (Bell, 2007: 11) of her surroundings. They take up what is to hand and what is particular to the site—particular knowledges that she and the students have, languages, materials for drawing, writing and reading, storytelling practices, printing presses, the diverse spaces of the room, the other people who work with them. There are glimpses of movement and invention. The classroom is a space where smooth and striated spaces coincide. This account indicates that these striations exceed the bodies and the walls of the classroom as the pedagogical encounter includes places and people beyond the classroom—from the desert families to which students return in Toyotas at the end of semester, through the school nurse and the Aboriginal teacher-mentor to broad institutional structures of governance and regulation including the Catholic church and Commonwealth government who had responsibility at this time for Aboriginal education yet who are marked by their absence in the text. Institutional neglect is evidenced by the health impacts on students— students with trachoma and lice. The removal of children for schooling from towns and communities where adequate education and healthcare are not available also suggests institutional neglect.

We say sorry

Pedagogical encounters are not divorced from space or time and the account in the previous section indicates that although we might theoretically undo categories of difference such as race there are profound and persistent material effects from the imposition of these categories. The practice that Bell calls "chaining" where subjects are attached to historically and socially situated categories provides one way of understanding "embodied relations to the past," their political effects in the present and their erratic trajectories into the future (Bell, 2007: 32). Although categories of racial difference including "Aboriginal" are contingent and performative they can also be purposeful as they are taken up by subjects who locate themselves relative to these categories.

The story in the previous section indicated the entanglements of history within which the young teacher and her students were bound. The "national story" also, inevitably, contains and shapes the subjects within the nation who are differently positioned within it. In the early 1980s, the plates on which the teacher and her students are located are beginning to shift. They are located on a map that they cannot see, and whose coordinates they do not know. It is impossible to consider this story now without taking into account what has and hasn't happened for indigenous people and between indigenous and non-indigenous Australians in the years since the young teacher landed with those children in that room in north-western Australia. Pedagogical encounters are "always mediated" and presuppose "other faces, other encounters of facing, other bodies, other spaces and other times" (Ahmed, 2000: 7). The third story about difference in this chapter is an excerpt from the 2008 speech that opened the first Parliament headed by the then new Prime Minister Kevin Rudd. This speech, broadcast live around the nation to large screens and gathered crowds, from public parks to primary schools, can itself be understood as a pedagogical encounter on a national scale.

The nation had recently emerged from eleven years of official disparagement of what was dismissed as a "black-arm-band view of history" by ex-Prime Minister John Howard. One of the first acts of the new government was an official apology in the Federal Parliament, an act long overdue in the eyes of many Australians. The story in the previous section reaches across an enormous gulf in recent Australian history and resonates with the Prime Minister's speech in its position on responsibility and the ethics of encounter. The work of Levinas suggests that responsibility entails abandoning the autonomous and independent self in favor of a necessary interdependence. For Levinas, emerging from the deep shadows of the European holocaust, responsibility for others had to be "not only absolute and unconditional, but it is the very condition of possibility for subjectivity and identity...one is hostage to the other" (Ahmed, 2000: 146). Ahmed argues that despite the infinitude of responsibility, it is the "*the finite and particular circumstances in which I am called on to respond to others*" that make an ethical encounter (Ahmed, 2000: 147). The "I" that Ahmed evokes is of critical importance because within Levinasian ethics, responsibility "can only ever be attributed to the self, the singular subject" (Todd, 2003: 109). The burden of responsibility cannot be entirely passed on to an abstract body like "government" or to an institution. It is noteworthy that in the apology to the stolen generation that began the first term of the new Australian federal government on February 13th, 2008, the Prime Minister used both singular and plural first person pronouns to speak the words of the apology to the nation:

> For the pain, suffering and hurt of these Stolen Generations, their descendants and for their families left behind, *we say sorry*. To the mothers and the fathers, the brothers and the sisters, for the breaking up of families and communities, *we say sorry*. And for the indignity and degradation thus inflicted on a proud people and a proud culture, *we say sorry*...To the Stolen Generations, I say the following: as Prime Minister of Australia, *I am sorry*. On behalf of the Government of Australia, *I am sorry*. On behalf of the Parliament of Australia, *I am sorry*. (Rudd, 2008, italics added)

In the Prime Minister's speech the rhetorical movement from "We say" to "I am" represents a significant ontological shift. The verb moves from "to say," which captures the necessary and public gesture of speaking out aloud the word that his predecessor refused to use, to the verb "to be" in the latter part of the speech. In the part of the speech where he says "I am," Rudd folds the surface performance of saying sorry, into himself. It is the "I am sorry" that carries through the affective ripple of the apology that has begun earlier in the speech with "We say sorry." The "we" of the Prime Minister's speech includes successive governments, but it also includes the people elected to parliament, the thousands of Australians who trekked to Parliament House in Canberra for the event and many of the millions who watched the broadcast across the nation. The "we" also brings into being a category that can encompass "these Stolen Generations, their descendants and...the families left behind...mothers and fathers...brothers and sisters." The shift to "I am sorry" suggests that responsibility is also always tied to the singular subject. And the call to the other entailed in an ethical encounter is populated by specific and particular subjects. Rudd weaves part of his speech around the experience of a single woman, taken from her family almost eighty years ago, her story emblematic of, but not identical to, the stories of any of the other "up to 50,000 children" stolen from their families during the recent history of the Australian nation.

In the context of the Prime Minister's apology to indigenous Australians and the long refusal to apologies of his predecessor, the responsibility evokes further responses at individual and national levels. For people who take themselves up as Aboriginal, the performance of and repetition of difference is instrumental in reconciliation politics and is a strategy adopted for pedagogical and political purposes. In a recent article in the national magazine *The Monthly*, Galarrwuy Yunupingu, leader of the Gumatj clan of Arnhem land and past Australian of the Year, insists on the multiplicity of indigenous difference as he lists "the great clan nations of the Gove Peninsula: Rirritjingi, Djapu, Wanguri, Djalwong, Mangalili, Malarrpa, Marrakulu, Dartiway, Naymil, Gumatj, Galpu, Djumbarrpiynu, Dhudi-Djapu" (2008: 34). Yunupingu's iteration of these names for a predominantly urban Anglo-Australian readership can be understood as a performative gesture that is "contingent, contextualized, intermittent and temporal" (Bell, 2007: 36). Many people belong to multiple clan groups through complex relationships that transcend biological genealogies. Yunupingu, in his evocation of the clan nations and his insistence on multiplicity, has educative and political intent.

The Prime Minister's speech can be understood as a pedagogical encounter on a national scale that opens up a space of becoming and that is oriented to the future and the possibility of "new kinds of society and new people" (Patton, 2007: ix). It seemed to open—in that moment—a new line of flight for the millions of viewers from the habituated modes of thinking that had become sedimented through the previous regime. This chapter also explored the notion of the ethical encounter in the spaces and places of schooling. In these classrooms, in some moments, teacher and students inhabited an "intermezzo" marked by "the dynamics of experience, activity, or even feeling as an ongoing process of creation and becoming" (Stivale, 1998: 2).

It examined how we might understand classrooms and their curious social and material boundaries. The classrooms in this chapter were spaces that were both physical and social spaces and were simultaneously permeable and contained arenas for encounters. Although teachers tend to have a strong sense that this is "my classroom" and my class, and students likewise tend to have a strong sense of themselves as part of a coherent and recognizable place, these communities are leaky organisms. Their boundaries seep and the locations of inside(rs) and outside(rs)— and inside and outside knowledges—are much less fixed than is usually anticipated. Pedagogy emerges from an ethical encounter of particular people in a particular place and time, and are contingent on the diverse and particular knowledges that they bring with them into that space, and that come to hand there. Pedagogy is necessarily enacted and socially situated. And it happens within spaces that are themselves "living participants in the enactive moment" (Roy, 2005: 29). The pedagogical assemblage that the teacher co-creates with her students—planning and preparation, resources, texts generated in class, languages, modes of organizing furniture, funneling movement, "managing" space, time and behavior—are each particular to a classroom, a school, a group of students, a specific historical and "geo-ontological moment" (Roy, 2005: 29). Likewise the Prime Minister's staging of his historic speech of apology and his use of the vast resources of the media who simultaneously broadcast his speech live around the nation to waiting crowds emerged in a particular spatial and temporal plane of possibility. Yunupingu's evocation of the clan nations of Arnhem land and their demand for a treaty is another intervention located in particular space and time and his use of national media to broadcast this demand becomes possible in relation to the Prime Minister's speech as well as a range of previous events.

In school education difference is also often understood in terms of racial otherness. Discourses of diversity tend to categorize people into ethnic and raced identities that elide many other differences amongst the subjects of such discourses. Ahmed suggests that difference is most often understood as an optic effect, predicated on the visual appearance of difference (Ahmed, 2000: 107). These have underpinned institutional processes of racialization, exclusion and disadvantage for decades in this nation and elsewhere. Binaries of racial difference can leave naïve categories of difference unchallenged and can obscure the hybrid and multiple identities that are patched together by contemporary subjects as they move through the diverse domains of their lives. Shifting to an ethics of pedagogical encounter brings an insistence on the specificity of each encounter and the particularity of each subject in an encounter. It is particularity rather than generalization that contributes to an ethical encounter, an encounter that has the possibility of transcendence and can call forth an inexorable responsibility for the other.

Although responsibility emerges from the ethical encounter with a particular other, Prime Minister Rudd's statement of apology to the stolen generations also demonstrates that this does not preclude nor evade the responsibility for many others who have suffered injustice and violence at the hands of governments and individuals. Difference is also, always, inflected by relative differentials of power and privilege that cannot be overlooked. The Prime Minister's speech provided an opportunity for ethical encounters for people around the nation. At the University of Western Sydney, for example, the live broadcast was watched by people, gathered by open invitation, at the Vice Chancellor's building, including staff, students, aboriginal elders and youth from the Dharug nation. The Prime Minister's speech was framed by speeches from the Vice Chancellor and an Aboriginal elder. People stood side by side—and face to face—and were moved to tears and to apologies that rippled on and on after the large screen was turned off. There was a sense of transcendence and the notion that had been promulgated by the previous government that "they cannot be held responsible for actions that they have not themselves committed" was, in that encounter, undone (Todd, 2003: 94). This was however just the first step on the road to what can only ever be partial reparations.

And so...

The stories in this chapter have attempted to work against naturalized and dominant modes of understanding difference through fixed categories of identity. Analysis has focused on the moment of the pedagogical encounter, the face to face instant of student and students, and teacher and students in the odd little neighborhoods of particular classrooms. It has explored, in relation to these instances, whether and to what extent ethical encounters are possible in secondary schooling. Furthermore, in this chapter I have introduced several public pedagogical events and examined the extent to which these manifest elements of ethical encounter across difference. The chapter has added Levinas, through Ahmed, Bell and Todd, into the theoretical assemblage informed by Deleuze that underpins this book.

In the next chapter, reinforcing the point that learning takes place in diverse settings, Catherine and Constance analyze their experiences as adult students in a community education context. They write of a process that was experienced as transformative, of opening themselves to differenciation in community in the space of an alternative drama class.

Notes

[i] Thanks to Peter Bansel for his discussion of the notion of "coagulation."

5
BECOMING BLOSSOM, BECOMING ODDBOD: CLOWNING AS TRANSFORMATIONAL PROCESS
CONSTANCE ELLWOOD AND CATHERINE CAMDEN PRATT

The place

This chapter explores the pedagogies that were opened up in an informal adult learning space, in which both authors had, at different times, and unknown to each other at that time, been students. The stories-so-far that we tell in this chapter, arose in the collective biography workshop when we focused on learning spaces that were "responsive and transformable" (Ceppi and Zini, 1998: n.p.), and in which we had experienced opportunities to open up to new ways of learning, being and becoming. We reflected on contexts in which acts of self-learning had been "constructed, deconstructed, and consolidated as a result of exchange and relations with others" and on the ways in which this context had determined "the possibilities and qualities of the learning processes" (Ceppi and Zini, 1998: n.p.).

This reflection, in the collaborative context of this book, enables both a movement back—historically and autobiographically—but also forward, as we look again at our stories through the lenses provided by Deleuze and by the Reggio Emilia philosophy. This re-viewing enables us to see the past differently, and in so doing to engage in the present in a new process of differenciation, opening up to difference in a way that "produces life itself, and enables the production of the new" (Hickey-Moody and Malins, 2007: 5).

Drama Action Centre, DAC, was a privately-run "fringe" drama school which existed in Sydney over a seventeen-year period in the 1980s and 1990s. Categorizing itself as a Theatre of Movement and as "being open to anyone interested in discovering or furthering their artistic expression" (Brandon and Batten, 1984: n.p.), DAC offered a wide range of performance and theatre-related skills. "Being open to anyone" meant that DAC attracted an eclectic range of people. The students' ages ranged from their early twenties to their late fifties, and possibly older. There were students of theatre and television, office workers, singers, teachers, lawyers, accountants, brothers and nuns from religious orders, as well as women who identified primarily as mothers. While many students went on to make a name for themselves in various kinds of mainly non-mainstream theatre, for others, the focus was on, in the language of the time, personal growth.

Described as "a conduit for new ideas and practice" (O'Connor, 2001: 47), DAC was actively and overtly a space for becoming, for processes of de-individualization and the constitution of new ways of being. Classes in mask, movement, dance, mime, improvisation, clowning, chorus and performance provided the tools for these becomings which were supported by certain sets of practices, by the community of learners, and by the context.

In order to critically reflect on the authors' collective biography stories, we first describe and discuss the historically specific practices and approaches taken at DAC.

The practices

The teaching at DAC drew on the psychodramatic techniques of Jacob Moreno (1953). Psychodrama uses drama and role play to explore issues and concerns of individuals, groups and organizations. It is most commonly used as a group method, in which each person in the group becomes a transformative agent for the others. Moreno saw psychodrama's key function as the development of (appropriate forms of) spontaneity which in turn enabled greater creativity within systems, be they the system of an individual or of a group (Fox, 1987; Holmes, 1991; Schacht, 2007). Moreno's psychodrama is directed toward the discovery of new solutions and approaches to old problems. It can be seen therefore as a pragmatic approach to addressing what Foucault called the need to "think differently, instead of legitimating what is already known" (Foucault, 1992: 9).

The discovery of new solutions and approaches to old problems was further enabled through the application of group theory (see for example Bion, 1961). A group theory approach recognizes the importance of processes within the group, and of the relationships between and among group members, including links between individuals, the function of the "star" member, and processes of inclusion and exclusion. Attention to group processes was a key strategy employed in this space. The result was a dynamic community in which many strong connections were forged and which manifested "a form and quality of the space that fosters encounters, exchange, empathy and reciprocity" (Ceppi and Zini, 1998: n.p.). This sense of community could be seen in its apotheosis in the chorus work section of the DAC curriculum, a process in which the aim was to develop the ability for the whole group to become co-extensive with others and to literally move as one.

Psychodramatic approaches, underpinned by the application of group theory, worked alongside theatre training strategies, particularly those of Jacques LeCoq, to challenge the habits of thought and behavior that had sedimented within individuals' ways of living in the world. For LeCoq, the goal was to train students—largely through the tool of improvisation—to be capable not only of ease in theatrical performance but also of ease in life. "My hope," he once wrote, "is for my students to be consummate livers of life and complete artists on stage" (LeCoq, Carasso and Lallias, 2001: 18). Improvisation, which works on the principle of accepting and extending on "offers" from oneself, others and objects, includes an ability to "observe how beings and objects move, and how they find a reflection in us" and is at the heart of a process which enables people "to discover themselves in relation to their grasp of the external world" (LeCoq et al., 2001: 19). LeCoq's theatre training was in some ways "an education in seeing" within a univocal world, where performance involved a dialogic "act of creation" in which the performer's ego "is superfluous," but where both performer and spectator receive pleasure from the performance (LeCoq et al., 2001: 19). LeCoq's approach is echoed in the Reggio Emilia attention to listening as a highly interactive process. It is not about "monologic transmission" but is rather a "radical dialogue" (Dahlberg and Moss, 2005: 101) where the participants enter a space together and together make meaning. For LeCoq, performance, through improvisation, is therefore not simply about self-expression. It implies handing something on to the public/the Other; it is "a fruit which...separates from the tree" (LeCoq et al., 2001: 18). In its recognition of the other, this type of performance is highly ethical. "To be responsible for the other is also, at the same time, to respond to the other, to speak to her, and to have an encounter in which something takes place" (Ahmed, 2000: 147). It also echoes Deleuze's comment about reading with love:

> [T]he only question is 'Does it work, and how does it work?' How does it work for you?...something comes through or it doesn't...It's like plugging in to an electric circuit...it relates a book directly to what's Outside...This intensive way of reading, in contact with what's outside the book, as a flow

meeting other flows, one machine among others, as a series of experiments for each reader in the midst of events that have nothing to do with books, as tearing the book into pieces, getting it to interact with other things, absolutely anything...is reading with love. (Deleuze, 1995: 7-9)

Together, psychodrama, group theory, and LeCoq's approach to theatre training created contexts for interactions in which knowledge of oneself could be "constructed, deconstructed and consolidated as a result of exchange and relations with others" (Ceppi and Zini, 1998: n.p.) and in which were opened up possibilities for pushing beyond both personal and social norms. DAC practices thus worked toward enabling new ways of being in the world, "metamorphosing new bodies from old through their encounter" (Grosz, 2001: 70). This process aligns with the Deleuzian concepts of becomings and of lines of flight. Lines of flight offer "a productive, affirmative, and positive dynamism pointing to the nexus of change" (Albrecht-Crane and Slack, 2007: 102). Lines of flight are moved along by affective connections and there always exists some kind of becoming which results from exposure to/encounters with others, such that "affects are becomings" (Deleuze and Guattari, 1987: 256). The outcomes of the metamorphosis are by definition unknown; a line of flight carries us "towards a destination which is unknown, not foreseeable, not pre-existent" (Deleuze and Parnet, 1987: 125). Importantly, becomings involve a production of the real. "The great and only error lies in thinking that a line of flight consists of fleeing from life; the flight into the imaginary, or into art. On the contrary, to flee is to produce the real, to create life, to find a weapon" (Deleuze and Parnet, 1987: 49).

The process

There was a focus at DAC on what the individual brings to the pedagogical context; the DAC brochure refers to "participants discover[ing] the artist in themselves," to "finding your own symbolic language of communication and imagery," to "the finding and liberating of each person's own spontaneous and particular clown," "developing the responsive thinking body" and to exploring "dream, archetypes and mythic realities both personal and social" (Brandon and Batten, 1984: n.p.). The approaches of finding, liberating and discovering refer to challenges to the archive of each individual, which, over time, has sedimented as truths-of-the-self but, which, through dramatic techniques such as improvisation, are now highlighted as no-longer-possible ways to be. The responsive thinking body develops through encounters with and in response to these sedimentations. The process is one of exploration of the self, and of the mythic realities of the self, as produced by society.

In Deleuzian terms the process involved differenciation, in which internal processes of differentiation occur as the individual becomes other than itself. "A body is produced through an internal differenciation (as when cells differentiate) and, over time, continually differs from itself" (Hickey-Moody and Malins, 2007: 5). The productive nature of this differenciation process links to the idea that "difference is that which produces life itself" (ibid.: 5). In other words, as our stories will demonstrate, DAC's teaching practices drew on the transformative power of this internal process of differenciation to enable the becomings of students.

The challenges to and differenciation of the sedimented self took place within a community of learners whose responsiveness to, and sense of responsibility toward, others in the group had been developed through psychodramatic techniques and the application of group theory. It was a "conscious and capable management of contradictions and conflicts" (Ceppi and Zini, 1998: n.p.) in which each meeting with an other, or with no-longer-possible aspects of the sedimented self, was contained within the crucible of community. The processes of differenciation at DAC echo those of Kiet and Georgiy in Chapter Three, where a community of learners was built through the teacher's belief in, and practices toward fostering, each child's capacity for internal differenciation. That Kindergarten community managed "contradictions and conflicts" in such a way that the children in the room were able to safely enfold the emergent other in Kiet, while Georgiy was able to explore, if only briefly, that possibility of otherness in himself.

As in the Kindergarten classroom, a "strategy of attention" from all participants, both teacher and students, was key at DAC. It involved, above all, listening: "Listening as sensitivity to the patterns which connect, to that which connects us to others...with all our senses" (Rinaldi, 2006: 65). It was not, however, a compliant or complacent listening. As was suggested earlier in this book, an "empathetic context for listening" is a complex notion. At DAC, "empathy" had at times a firmer edge, when the student was provoked to confront, rather than withdraw from, the more challenging aspects of their archived histories and their sometimes dysfunctional modes of interaction. The process needed to be agonistic, since, as Deleuze says, we cling to "[o]ur security, the great molar organization that sustains us,...the binary machines that give us a well-defined status,...the system of overcoding that dominates us—we desire all that" (1987: 227). Here, a certain violent disruption of the overcoded self was sometimes seen as a precondition for learning but it was a "violence which is necessary to the formation of the subject" (Todd, 2003: 18). For the student, this process "demands that we have clearly in mind the value of the unknown and that we are able to overcome the sense of emptiness and precariousness that we experience whenever our certainties are questioned" (Rinaldi, 2006: 65).

LeCoq refers to the teacher's role here as making "simple observations, placed at the service of a living structure" (LeCoq et al., 2001: 20).

> My first response to any performer's improvisation or exercise is to make observations, which are not to be confused with opinions...One must pay close attention to the living process, while trying to be as objective as possible. The critical comments one makes about the work do not attempt to distinguish the good from the bad, but rather to separate what is accurate and true from what is too long or too brief, what is interesting from what is not. This might appear pretentious but the only thing which interests us is what is accurate and true: an artistic angle, an emotion, a color combination. (LeCoq et al., 2001: 19)

The role of the teacher in this pedagogy is, through attending to affect, emotion, the body and its movement, and the physical objects that have become extensions of the performative self, to recognize and affirm the "accurate and true" in the student's performance and to set it free. As Deleuze states, "to affirm is not to take responsibility for, to take on the burden of what is, but to release, to set free what lives" (Deleuze, 1983: 185).

Such "experimentation in contact with the real" (Deleuze and Guattari, 1987: 12) was made possible because DAC's practices and emotional environment enabled space for things to open up. Not only was the classroom space "responsive and transformable" in its capacity to contain the huge variety and levels of skill covered in the course—as students moved from basic skills to performance—but also in its capacity to contain the deconstruction and reconstruction processes undergone by individuals within the group and by the group as a unit.

Second skins

At DAC, a non-academic setting, the conscious application of the principles of group theory and the connections it forged worked to form a kind of second skin within which differenciation could occur; it provided an alchemical crucible for transformation. In addition to this, another layer of "skin" was created by the physical place itself. The DAC hall[i] was set amidst unkempt gardens in the grounds of what had once been a property of over 100 acres on the Parramatta River settled in the 1830s by an early colonist. Many of the features of the propertied classes—wrought iron gates, pergolas, and ponds—still remained. Historically the grounds had been used as a site for psychiatric hospitals from 1876—this included Callan Park (1876-1976), Broughton Hall (1921-1976) and, from 1976, Rozelle Psychiatric Hospital. At the time of the DAC classes, the property was dotted with numerous buildings of uncertain origin, some still in use in a mental health capacity, and some in use by community organizations such as DAC. Like the trees and shrubs which surrounded the DAC hall, most of the buildings had experienced some neglect. The DAC hall itself was a large old high-ceilinged, musty-smelling, wooden-floored building with a weed-filled water feature at its entrance.

A phantom presence of colonialists and psychiatric patients, of questionable and abjected history, was still present in the material evidence of neglect and decay. A sense of nostalgia evoked by the remnants of white Australia's historical past, alongside the abandoned buildings and tangled gardens, evoked, as if in opposition to the past, a new and as-yet-undiscovered future. At the same time, the rich sensory experience of the wilderness of uncontrolled nature in the unkempt gardens evoked life at its most basic and inchoate, un-colonized and uncontrolled. Overall, then, there was a sense of possibility, of lack of constraint and of the un-regimented, where previous striations of status and order, and the monstrous control of non-normative subjects, had been over-written by smooth space—a space full of possibilities for transformation. In this sense, the physical environment generated an "energy giving second skin" (Ceppi and Zini, 1998: n.p.) which facilitated deconstruction, openness to change, and spontaneity.

Additionally, within the DAC classes, the use of theatrical props provided a more literal second skin. Masks: neutral, clown and commedia dell' arte; costumes: velvet gowns, tutus, baggy pants, suspenders, furs; and other objects: balls, hoops, balloons, pegs, ribbons, bags, walking sticks and much else: all became part of this visible second skin, as did movements, music, gestures, percussive sounds, facial expressions and bodily contortions.

A further way in which the concept of second skin worked here, for the author of our first story, was in a deeply personal connection with the place. Her mother had been hospitalized in this psychiatric facility before the author was born. As a child she had visited her mother in Gladesville Psychiatric Hospital, which was on the opposite side of the Parramatta River and a very similar site to this one. This second skin held a number of complex memories of the challenges of growing up with a mother with a mental illness (see Camden-Pratt, 2006, 2002). At the time of her story, given below, the author had not revealed this aspect of her history to the DAC community.

Our two stories illustrate the possibilities which were opened up in this crucible of place, psychodrama, group processes, theatre tools and a carefully elaborated strategy of attention. Both stories relate the experience of participating as a clown. In the first story, the clown is yet to be "found," and the "finding" process is a painful one as the author struggles to stay with the "accurate and true" in the process of discovering herself in relation to her "grasp of the external world" (LeCoq et al., 2001: 19).

Finding Blossom

I stand in front of the row of chairs—my classmates sit with clown noses on elastic around their necks. I am thirty-four and in the process of leaving my thirteen-year marriage. "Now, put on your nose." Bridget's voice is warm and firm. It is Week One of our twelve-week term in clowning at the Drama Action Centre's two-year part-time Drama Course. I pull the round red plastic mask up from my neck and place it on my nose. I look out from my eyes. My classmates and Bridget look back. "Just let your clown emerge." The minutes pass. I feel heat rising. Tears begin to gather silently. I am on fire. I move to sit down. "You have ten minutes, you cannot sit down." Her voice cuts across the air, tender, clear, unmoving. I look at my classmates. I am a rabbit stuck in the headlights. My throat surges. My stomach swells. I swallow hard. I hold my breath until I cannot hold it any longer. I breathe high and shallow, my stomach reverberates. I gulp shuddering sobs. My red nose fills. I look at my classmates, at Bridget. "Five more minutes, you cannot sit down." I cannot stop crying, wailing. I look out through my lake-filled eyes, my ears pop. My classmates look back; they shift from one buttock to the other. I see Anna has tears. "All right, you can sit down now, well done."

Over the next ten weeks we practice running, tumbling, cart wheeling, trick-falling across the space, improvising alone and in pairs with umbrellas and hula hoops, balls and bags. Each week after the tea break we sit in our row and one after the other we stand, clown mask on, and face the group. Each week I hold my breath tight. I tell myself, "I am not going to cry this week." I feel my classmates willing me not to cry. I stand, I pull my clown nose up over my own and I stand sparse, bare, silent, no laughter, no cartwheels or wisecracks. I look at my classmates. I scan their faces. I search their eyes.

Each week I feel the steady rise of cries from somewhere lost inside me and I close my throat against them. I try to hold strong, to conquer my tears. Each week the moment arrives and I cannot contain my shuddering sobs. I stand alone, witnessed, my nose fills and I cannot breathe inside or out. "Can't she sit down?" Michelle asks Bridget in Week Five. "No, ten minutes—then she can sit down—she's doing well." I watch my classmates' clowns emerge. Clown masks on, they, by turns, are cheeky, poke faces, spin cartwheels, pretend to trip over their feet and pull magic rabbits from imaginary hats. I cannot bear my failure and yet I cannot not come to class. Each week I decide I won't go anymore until it's almost time to leave home and then I decide I will, rushing now because I'm late.

In Week Ten we are to come to class with a clown name, an outfit and a song. All week I decide I will not go anymore. I am angry with an uncomfortable rage I do not understand. I am trapped with no way out that I want to take. I am driven by an unarticulated desire for transformation: I want to come to the end of my sadness; I want to find joy. I want to play like the child I have never been. I arrive late; the hall is busy with my classmates dressing up in their clown outfits. Anna is in a cleaner's outfit, bucket and mop. Sigrid has a bag of pegs and her hair tied in a scarf. Josh is dressed in shorts with suspenders and a little boy's school hat and tie. Gareth is all color, his hair full of rainbows. Bridget meets me with a welcoming smile, "Quickly, get dressed we're about to start." "I haven't brought anything. I don't have a clown," I scowl. Bridget scans my empty hands. "There's a dressing room behind the stage, get something from there." I begin to protest. "Now" she says, her warm clear brown eyes holding mine. I drag my feet, muttering, "But I don't have a clown."

The dressing room smells of mothballs and sweat. It's full of old clothes on hangers, shoes and handbags in green garbage bags, walking sticks and hats in old fruit boxes. I look around, pull things out of bags and throw them on the floor. I turn to leave—at least I've looked. My eyes catch a glimpse of a dirty pink ribbon poking out of a torn garbage bag. I pull out the jumpers at the top and find a dirty pointe shoe. *My breath catches, I scrabble furiously through the bag, there's got to be another one, I can't find it, I empty the bag onto the floor and the missing shoe drops out among cardigans and a pair of red platform shoes from the seventies. I sit down, they fit me, I rise up onto my* pointes *and* pas de bourrée *across the floor, I do changements in second position and a pirouette. "It's time!" Bridget calls from the front of stage. I look around me, my clown needs a dress, I scan the racks. A dirty white nylon house gown draws me and I try it on—perfect fit. I find a blue nylon scarf and emerge from the behind the stage. My feet now penguin walking in* pointe *shoes, my hair tied back off my face with the blue nylon scarf, my body shapeless in the dirty nylon house coat with loose threads where some buttons are missing. I sit in the row with my classmates.*

Finally it's my turn. I put on my clown nose and I stand. "What's your name?" Bridget asks "I don't have a name," I say, standing silent. "What do you think?" she asks the group, "can we help her with a name?" They suggest a few that just don't fit, then Anna says "Blossom, what about Blossom?" I rise on my pointes *and* pas de bourrée *in a circle, my arms stretched out gracefully in my house coat, "Yes," I say, "I'm Blossom." "What's your song, Blossom?" asks Bridget. I am silent, my legs strong, my body slender under the dirty old coat, my feet arched perfectly high on my* pointes. *I open my mouth, my voice rises and falls on my breath and the words escape into the hall, "Somewhere over the rainbow, way up high, there's a land that I dreamed of once in a lullaby." I sing to the end of my song, clear and unwavering, and stop, my words echoing in the silence that follows. I am shaking. My lost dreams of becoming a ballerina stir in me and I feel into the second-hand housewife's coat that has become my life.*

The author finds herself caught for ten weeks in an in-between space—not-yet clown but also not not-clown; after all she is wearing the mask that signifies clown. Although she weeps and feels an uncomfortable rage, she also recognizes the "space of movement, of development, and of becoming" (Springgay, 2008: 27). The steady insistence by the facilitator on ten minutes is part of an attempt to "free expression to create new combinations" (Roy, 2004: 309). Its seeming striation provides "the conditions under which something new might be produced" (Reynolds and Webber, 2004: 2) and is "the small plot of land" (Deleuze and Guattari, 1987: 161) from which experimentation and the potentials of deterritorialization can be tried out. The *pointe* shoes also provide this small plot of land; the world of ballet is a world the author recognizes and in which she had herself been recognized in the past. The shoes function as a safe territory, both literally and metaphorically, from which the becoming body gains "the necessary strength or resolve to head out into the world" (Hickey-Moody and Malins, 2007: 11).

The student clown's unarticulated desire for transformation and her wanting to find joy are intimations of a line of flight; they are the flow beneath the social codes instilled in her not only through traumatic childhood experiences including her mother's mental illness but also through all the social structures that mould and shape us all into suitable social beings:

> Lines of flight are instantiations of desire, the primal force upon which society is built. As such, they form a productive, affirmative, and positive dynamism pointing to the nexus of change. Desire, according to Deleuze and Guattari, is critical; it names that force that breaks up the reductive molar workings of social organizations. (Albrecht-Crane and Slack, 2007: 102)

The expansion, extension and expression made possible in such creative practices, within the context of softness and relationality—Bridget's warm clear brown eyes, her warm voice, her welcoming smile—and the trust in the possibilities of the line of flight all take place within a community and among practices which work to maximize "the capacities of all bodies to affect and be affected...affirming difference and the production of the new" (Hickey-Moody and Malins, 2007: 4). As we saw in Chapter Two with the teacher Jo, this is not a process of conscious individual change in which a unitary subject is separate and isolated from others, but it is a process in which relationality, or being-with, is crucial. The non-unitariness of the subject can be seen, for example, in Anna. In Week One, Anna, as audience member, mirrors the tears in the performer's eyes, and, in Week Ten, proposes the name, "Blossom." This is the sense of a community of "exchange, empathy and reciprocity" which recognizes the interactions between bodies and their affects, rather than according total power to any one sovereign individual (Ceppi and Zini, 1998: n. p.).

This process can be seen as highly ethical, resting as it does on openness and recognition (Braidotti, 2006; Butler, 2004). It is a process of working toward "the well-being of an enlarged sense of community" (Braidotti, 2006: 35). At the same time, it is a process for the student clown of knowing that, however inarticulable, these tears have a meaning for her, that there is something "accurate and true," and that, however painful the experience is, she is partaking of an "experiment with the real" (Deleuze and Guattari, 1987: 12).

In re-viewing this story as part of the collective biography, the author saw how she drew on her learning at DAC to later establish classroom environments (see Chapter Three) in which differenciation was possible in a context of overall softness using relationality as modeled by Bridget in this story. Her capacity to trust the intelligence of self-learning at the edges of chaos as she experienced her self be-coming Blossom later enabled her to trust Kiet's and Georgiy's own self-learning in spite of her fears in the face of the molar and constraining line of force embodied in the principal. She recognized Kiet and Georgiy as being engaged with something "accurate and true" and that they were indeed "experimenting with the real" just as she had needed to do in the process of her student clowning in order to find Blossom. This re-viewing showed her how her lines of flight and their outcomes in an adult learning context had been re-territorialized into her pedagogical practices as a teacher.

Being Oddbod

In our second story, the clown, about to go on stage to perform to strangers, is no longer in the safe crucible of the DAC community. The clown has been "found," having come into being through similar processes to those described in the first story. Nevertheless, his/her ontological status is still uncertain and fragile, and the listening capacity of this audience, their strategy of attention, is as yet unknown. The questions of whether this clown will "work," whether something will "come through" (Deleuze, 1995: 7), remains doubtful in the mind of the actor.

"It's your turn! You're on now!" Lyn urges. "But what shall I do?" I ask anxiously. "Just be Oddbod!" is the kindly bemused reply. "But who is Oddbod? What does Oddbod do?" becomes my silent internal mantra. No time for answers, as I run down the back lane toward the door into the courtyard. Behind the high wooden fence I can hear the audience

chattering and stirring. I am tense with nervousness, high heart-rate, throat gripped, palms moist, nauseous, icy cold.

I push at the door, nervously, unwilling. It sticks and then gives with a rush. Suddenly I am there, exposed to the many eyes, whose chatter falls away, and who watch silently, expectantly, as I pause at the threshold, unwilling to enter, uncertain how to do Oddbod. I look back at them; Oddbod looks back at them. Our eyes flick nervously, we wear a slight anxious frown.

We step over the threshold and walk gingerly, uncertainly, hesitatingly, into the centre of the space. Eyes flick for danger. Can these people be trusted? What are they expecting? Oddbod stands silently in the centre of the space, looking anxiously at the audience from under the brim of the battered hat. Waiting nervously. Wishing to be not there.

Time extends. And extends. The audience is silent, attentive, and, could it be, Oddbod wonders, even 'spellbound'? Every movement is closely observed: the nervous gestures of the hands, the cowed head, the flicking of the eyes, the shuffling feet, the backwards glances to the escape of the door. This is what Oddbod does.

I notice a few slight chuckles of recognition, increasing now as Oddbod continues to do nothing but stand there, nervously and fearfully. And I am thinking: they like this.

The fear lessens, Oddbod begins to settle and prepares to make an announcement, licks lips, opens mouth, closes mouth, opens mouth, wrings hands, opens mouth, closes mouth, eyes flick for safety, for escape. No. The fear has returned and Oddbod again looks silently and anxiously out at the audience, at the door, at the audience.

The chuckles are increasing in volume, I notice, and Oddbod begins to feel quite bold, looking back at the audience with a sudden flush of confidence and pride. An unexpected loud roar of laughter is startling though, and Oddbod shrinks momentarily, but the laughter has caught and now the whole audience, it seems, is rocking and screaming with laughter. Oddbod soaks in the laughter, looking surprised but rather pleased. Behind the laughter, I hear the bell for five minutes and know that my turn is over. Oddbod, now looking confidently at the audience, bows elaborately, pleased with such professionalism, and, looking nervously self-congratulatory, backs out the escape door.

In this story we again see the author in process in an in-between space in which there is a metamorphosis of "new bodies from the old through their encounter" (Grosz, 2001: 70). As the clown, Oddbod, and the more striated, but rejected, identifications of the author—the one who is unable to speak in public, the one who fears the public gaze—interact in the performance space, there is a process of differenciation, of de-individualization, "an escape to some degree from the limits of the individual" (Roffe, 2007: 43). As a result, new ways of being in the world are produced. The new way of being a subject, in this case, develops from the discovery, by Oddbod—and experienced by the author as Oddbod—of the okay-ness of fear, even the humor in it. Once again, in Ceppi's and Zini's terms (1998: n.p.), the community of "exchange, empathy and reciprocity"—manifesting here in the audience—functions to hold the author as she moves out onto the stage as Oddbod, into this new way of being.

The question of what is accurate and true is foregrounded here. Oddbod's fear of performance is utterly true for the performer behind the red nose, but all that is required for the clown to "succeed" with the audience is that Oddbod remain true to all that s/he is feeling and experiencing in relation to that fear. Oddbod's performance becomes "a fruit which...separates from the tree" (LeCoq et al., 2001: 18), "an encounter in which something takes place" (Ahmed, 2000: 147). The audience members see their own fears accurately mirrored and their laughter is the laughter of relief as they too experience with Oddbod the okay-ness of this fear. It is also the strategy of attention, provided by the audience, which allows Oddbod to feel okay with fear. Here the audience in its being-with functions as a psychic second skin, holding and witnessing Oddbod's public performance.

And so...

In both stories we see at work a dynamic pedagogy that does not fix its subjects in static, rigid identities, but opens up a space in which becoming can unfold through ongoing affective relations, between self and other, and within selves. This process of fluid becoming is a movement away from the static notions of self to which we cling. A key aspect of this is the focus on "offering no solutions...only...questions" (LeCoq et al., 2001: x). These questions provoke a liberation of what has been covered over with "our social masks of skill, education, authority and sophistication" (Wright, 2001: 80). Becoming clown thus involves a production of the real (Deleuze and Parnet, 1987: 49); it is about "playing the truth game" and recognizing that "[T]he less defensive one is, the less one tries to play a character, and the more one allows oneself to be surprised by one's own weaknesses, the more forcefully one's clown will appear" (LeCoq et al., 2001: 145, translation modified). In the act of finding the clown, our social masks fall away; that which is "accurate and true" and that which "works" is revealed.

In the next chapter we experiment with becoming students in an art classroom. Constance was unable to be present and so we invited Peter, who is a member of our research group, to join us. Staying with the possibilities opened up by different modes of learning that take their inspiration from the arts, we each chose one of our stories and work with it in a visual medium. Inspired by the account of Springgay of art making as emergent pedagogy (2008) and by the work of Grosz on art and its use of "sensations, affects, intensities as its mode of addressing problems" (2008a: 1). We were curious about the possibilities that the movement from words, our usual medium, towards art making would open up. In the individual accounts that we provide, we attempt to slow down and to document the art making process as each of us experienced it. We are particularly interested in tracing the materiality of the process, where the substances, or the matter, that was to hand, demanded particular responses from us that often worked against, or at least in quite a different way, to the rational or intellectual intentions with which we each began.

Notes

[i] Over its history, DAC was located in several different suburbs of Sydney. At the time the authors attended classes, it was located in this hall.

6
REFLECTIONS ON A DAY IN THE ART CLASS
BRONWYN DAVIES, KATERINA ZABRODSKA, SUSANNE GANNON, PETER BANSEL AND CATHERINE CAMDEN PRATT

In this chapter we tell a series of stories-so-far about an experiment in the art of becoming. These stories have no point or conclusion; they are not contained by explanations and they do not accomplish any final representation of the art works we engaged in. On this day of the workshop, two of our education students, Jade Vardon and Alicia Ball, themselves almost at the end of their process of becoming (qualified) teachers, agree to become our teachers. The workshop opens a space that enables us to put our linear stories and analytic strategies to one side, and to give ourselves over to the emergent process of art making.

In this experiment, we are each, in our different ways, vulnerable and afraid—in the face of our own lack of skill, and of the affective space we have given ourselves over to. Yet we are at the same time held safe by our young permission-giving teachers who move quietly among us, saving us by giving us new skills when we need them, lending us courage when we need it, offering specific ideas when our own imagination fails. Their calm quiet presence is never dominant or controlling. Rather, their strategy of attention allows us each to immerse ourselves in the process of art making, and to work through the affect that this work entails.

Deleuze's observation that differenciation is first and foremost individual is made evident in the deeply personal struggle that each of us engages in. Barely aware of each other, at times, we are, at the same time, held safe in the space of the art classroom, made up of rough wooden tables, used tubes of paint, a richness of objects to work with, and the quiet presence of the teachers and the other students—each engaged in their own works of art, each *with-the-other* in creating the space that makes the singular work possible.

> "...the abstractions of habit and memory militate against the emergence of new sensations and hence against the expression of virtual

> intensities and ideas...So do not make your variation depend on representation, habit and memory. Leave all actual things behind (forget everything)." (Williams, 2003: 5).

In our own small foray into art, we threw ourselves into the deep-end of our own unknowing. In what follows we try to lay bare each of our own moments of discovery, of becoming, in the art classroom. For each of us this is a very different process, each of us solving different problems, yet working together, creating a singular/plural sense of community, totally absorbed in our own spaces of becoming yet always also, in that very effort, members of the event that was unfolding.

Bronwyn's account

It was intriguing for me to give myself over to the emergent process of art making. The story I chose was the one of making a paper doll in an earlier collective biography workshop on embodied women at work (Davies and Gannon, 2006). I had no idea really what I would make, and was very aware of my lack of skill—and my desire to learn from Jade and Alicia. I had tried to think of images in the days beforehand that I would create, but failed to come up with anything definite. I brought with me lots of richly colored cloth, and richly colored paper—and thread and buttons—stuff I had chosen not to throw away over the years because it was beautiful.

When I looked at the board I was to work on it seemed too small. I covered it in a rich lapis blue and left it to one side. It seemed evident, then, that I would work with the cloth. The lush tropical trees that I had imagined as relevant to my story were not what I chose to work with, though I had constantly imagined them as my starting point. I began with the image of a second skin, and of layers. I decided to work with some beautiful light cobalt Thai silk, shot with red that I had bought ages ago—though it seems more accurate to say the cloth decided that I would use it. I hesitated a thousand times before I could bring myself to cut it, worrying about whether I needed to hem it or not, afraid of an error. I found a royal blue see-through scarf and pinned it over the top in voluptuous folds.

> "...in a fold, say in cloth, the outside is never fully absorbed. It is both at once exterior and interior...Deleuze translates the fold as sensuous vibrations, a world made up of divergent series; an infinity of pleats and creases." (Springgay, 2008: 5-6)

Onto the under-layer I pinned a square of gold cloth with bars on it to represent the veranda in my story, and three squares of white paper with a gold square in the middle, arranged like three ducks flying. Each square had a tiny bit of red in the corner. I cut out a blood-red silk teardrop and overlaid it on one of the squares. I thought I wanted several teardrops, but one was enough. The bloody teardrop was hidden behind the inside/outside folds of the veil. I sewed the squares and the teardrop onto the silk underneath. When I told Jade I thought the pleated block of gold silk that I pinned onto the under-layer was not adequately representing the veranda, she suggested I needed to find a way to link the veil with the under-surface and suggested stitching through all the layers to create a sense of the veranda rails. I couldn't bring myself to do that, as the veil needed to be able to float, so I cut the block of gold silk into bars to represent the veranda and sewed them on to the under-lying blue silk. Then I sewed three gold squares onto the veil that echoed and gave new energy to the flying squares underneath. I added a small spray of sequins, like flying foam. At that point I started to feel an intense joy.

But I knew I still had to cut the veil so the viewer could see through to the under-layer. I was deeply afraid that the cuts would be wrong. Jade listened to me talk about my fear, making it seem completely acceptable to be afraid. Then she asked was I ready to make the cut and stood calmly by while I made the first gash in the veil. Relief. But I knew I hadn't yet opened up the under-surface enough. Jade went off to help someone else. Then disaster struck. I made a bad cut. It was an ugly gash. The flow of the folds was hopelessly damaged. Trying to contain my panic, I tried cutting more and realized I was getting further into trouble not out of it. Jade calmly picked up two mother-of-pearl buttons from my button box and placed them on the wound showing how to draw the two sides together still revealing the under-layer, but containing and managing the cut. It was inspirational. I cut the wound further and sewed on the buttons. The crisis was past.

> "...our utopia should be in crisis! It should have the courage to be in crisis!...I am not dreaming about humanity having a final boundary or goal, but every moment can be thought of as a step...So we are not only working for some final goal, every moment has to find its own significance...Every moment is rich."
> (Rinaldi, 2006b: 202-3)

I couldn't have made it on my own as I had neither the skill nor the courage, but there it was, and it was beautiful. Katerina said it looked like a skirt. Catherine said it was me. What could that mean in terms of our process? Was there something that was recognizably "myself" that lay in this cloth, with its buttoned wound, its small splash of sequins, its hidden bloody teardrop, its hidden gold palings, its doubled sequence of gold squares in flight, its deep blueness, its presentation of itself as an integrated aesthetic whole, yet with bloody tears and wounds that were only visible for those who cared to look carefully. It wasn't "me" that I set out to represent. It was a free fall into my own affect, which included the joy of the original creation of the paper doll, and the complex scarification of being a woman in the academic workplace. It contained the deep blues of the tropical sea I loved so much, the glitter of early morning sun on sea water, and the pool of liquid gold on water in the setting sun. My "skirt," with its wound, revealed and hid the bloody teardrop, the visceral pain, the lines of flight, and the buttoned down restraint of women's bodies at work.

I had a little time left at the end of the day to play, so I turned to the blue board I'd painted, and painted on some curling waves and rocks and water spouting up and a rich golden sun. It contained elements of the first verse of the poem I'd written at the end of the Bombo workshop, when we each wrote down the words that most evoked our experience of being there in that space, and then each wrote a poem out of someone else's words. My poem was written out of Katerina's words:

> Possibilities of open space,
> of light on water,
> and women weeping,
> creeping out of their cocoons,

light, bright wings flashing
and whale tails thrashing
the deep blue surface of the sea.

My painting also included Catherine's sunny sun shining, and the angel wings of my chosen image from the original workshop I'd written my story about, and Peter's story about a child he had taught who had refused to climb a small, steep hill because she was afraid of touching the sky. It included the turbulence of the sea at Bombo and also the uplifting joy of waves and of working together, and the unexpected and erratic explosion of the waves in the Kiama blowhole that we had seen together. I found I could work quickly and without the fear of my first creation, remembering that Jade and Alicia had said it was OK to make mistakes, that the mistakes would be just another layer that could then turn into something else. That had been their starting point—you had to have layers that worked their way into being the thing you would arrive at— even if you didn't know where you were going. The skin of the painting could be multi-layered, and grow in richness and depth as you experimented with it, allowing it to emerge. The thing was to begin without too much fuss, and have courage to proceed, to trust the emergent process.

Katerina's account

When I had been invited to write my reflections on the day spent with my colleagues in the art class and especially on the process of translating our written stories to visual art, I felt a strange mixture of eagerness and resistance to doing so. It was an opportunity to transform my story once more, this time from the visual to the written form, and thus to reconstitute my experience through the written form that I am more comfortable working with. Yet, I also felt a profound dissatisfaction with my art work and was not at all sure whether it would be meaningful to dwell upon it. I was persuaded that what I had produced at the workshop was neither the visual counterpart of my collective biography story, nor something I intended to create. I thought that the art work was simply a misleading representation of the story, and I attributed this to my lack of skills and experience with art making. I felt a compelling need to improve my art work, so that it would become a more adequate embodiment of the story and of my emotions and thoughts related to it. While I still believe that the art work is something quite different from the story, I do not think that there is nothing to say about the process of its making.

I had been looking forward to the art class several weeks ahead. This was particularly because I genuinely appreciated and enjoyed the collective biography workshop and the company of its other participants. I had chosen to work with my story about the oppressive and alien second skin of the computer room at the national conference (Chapter Seven), and I had been keen to translate the anxiety and insecurity I felt while being there into visual art. A few days before the workshop, I had downloaded and printed dozens of pictures from the Internet, which I thought were evocative of my story. I especially liked diminutive, funny-looking photographs of some unfamiliar faculty members from my university. My plan had been to use them as a background for the whole art work. I had fantasized a space overfilled with images of very different kinds of people: there would be these weird, sulky and old-fashioned looking men, but also some ambitious young students in vivid colors, and perhaps even one amorous image to represent my boyfriend, who had distracted me considerably during my presentation in the conference room. This would be mixed with the black and white photographs of old, giant, mechanical computers. I also wanted to use a beautiful picture of a red horse from a recent Sydney Nolan exhibition, and some mysterious photographs of Foucault, all of which would represent a positive presence of the dangerous and the subversive within a powerful scientific tradition. My plan was to create a grim, oppressive collage with many different and orderly arranged layers representing disparate spaces and the disparate emotional valences of the conference room, together with a few disruptive and joyful spots.

At the art class, however, I somehow failed to actualize my vision. Or perhaps, quite the contrary, I actualized this vision in an exceedingly accurate way, but its effects differed greatly from what I had expected. When I reflect back on why I was not satisfied with my art work, I recognize that I had come to the art workshop with the vision perhaps too clear and tangible. I should not have planned so cautiously how to bring back to life my experience captured in the collective biography story. In attempting to represent my experience as adequately as possible, I made invisible to myself that "[t]he purpose of art is not to represent the world...but to create new and self-sufficient compositions of sensation, compositions that will draw those who experience them directly into the material vitality of cosmos itself" (Hallward, 2003: 72). I failed to remember that an artist can come closer to creative chaos and become "the liberator of creative anarchy in matter itself" (ibid.: 72). I am very much aware of the limits of a will to control a process of creation of specific objects or events, be they written or visual texts, a conversation, a perfect moment, or one's life. Still, this will is something which constitutes me as a subject and which I am invested in, despite my attempts to de(con)struct it.

The art work I finally created was an outcome of an attempt to duplicate the particular, well-defined vision of the conference room by more abstract means, and of my ignorance of how to work with visual art. After Alicia's and Jade's introduction (and despite their helpful suggestions of how we might start our work), I was at a complete loss. I wondered how to approach that white, blank canvas, which awaited me in the art classroom. I had not worked with visual art since my high school years and I had even forgotten how to begin to paint. After minutes of confusion and uncertainty, I looked at Bronwyn, who was already fully immersed in her painting, and realized that I needed to find a brush and some colors and to paint a foundation. I was taken aback by my lack of knowledge, which I had not been aware of. To make sure that I was doing the right thing and not some irreparable mistake, I asked Alicia to confirm for me my first step (a rather absurd thing to do, considering that it concerned only the foundation of the painting). I decided to use grey to depict the dim and gloomy second skin of the conference room. Afterwards, I was lost again. I aimed to work independently, but it turned out to be an unattainable goal, since I lacked the knowledge of how to use most of the materials and tools prepared for us. Alicia suggested that I try a new method utilizing wax, so that I would be able to create an image of walls covered with big signs saying SCIENCE, which I had brought with me. I spent some time working with wax, using a small knife to carve many copies of SCIENCE out of the waxed paper. As a result, I had tissue paper with SCIENCE, repeated and grandiose, painted with black ink. The signs appeared very artistic to me, but I was not sure how to use them. I wanted to glue them to the canvas in a specific way, which turned out to be impossible, so I let SCIENCE be for the moment. Then I saw a big piece of tin, which Alicia and Jade had brought, and decided to cut it to many different sized squares to represent the different material, symbolic and emotional spaces of the conference room.

At that point, I finally arrived at a distinct and realizable idea of how to abstractly represent the conference room and started to work on my canvas without any further breaks. I cut several tin squares and glued them to the grey canvas. The small squares symbolized different spaces of the room, but they could constitute people's heads or ideas too. The big piece of tin embodied the second skin of the room, and above all the rigor of science. I decided to write something on it. Alicia told me about an engraver and I learned how to use it after a while. I chose the most telling words from my story, such as "entirely covered with posters," "many more people," and "feel the gazes," and engraved them on the big tin square. Then I made use of a wooden place mat, which I had brought with me for no special reason. I cut it into long rectangles and glued them on the tin squares as a second layer of the canvas. I spent a lot of time trying different locations for every tin and wooden piece, to make sure that they were in the right place. After that I was fortunate enough to find a way to use some of the photographs I had brought. I took a computerized photo of Foucault, where he looked like a postmodern angel, and fastened it on one of the tin squares.

My work of art was almost finished: there were three layers of different materials and sizes, disparately but symmetrically placed on the grey foundation. Foucault was knowingly peering from one of the tin pieces as an icon of the new vision and the future. Still, the art work was too plain, and the feeling of oppression and crowdedness was not there. For a while, I pondered about completely covering the canvas with the tissue paper saying SCIENCE, but I realized that the paper was not transparent enough and that the canvas would not be seen through it. I was afraid that the whole work might be destroyed, so I abandoned this idea. But I still was not satisfied and decided to glue another piece of tin there, this time a long one with engraved indiscernible writing, so that it cut through many small tin pieces as a substitute for the tissue paper. I believed that the art work was completed, but then I remembered my red horse, cut out his eyes and glued them under the long piece of metal to represent a horrifying (and also somehow horrified) gaze of a scientific authority. After that I was content. Everything was there and it seemed to be quite an aesthetically pleasing piece of art.

It was when we started to discuss our works of art at the end of the day that I realized there was something wrong with what I had created. Before that, I had not looked much at other people's work because I was anxious that there was not enough time to finish my canvas and also because I knew that their art works were not ready for display yet. I was only aware that Bronwyn was working passionately on a beautiful, dark blue skirt and that Catherine was producing something dangerous, using long fair hair and drops of red looking like blood. Sue and Peter had been working in a different part of the art classroom and I was not sure what they were creating.

When we began to present our art works to each other, I was surprised to see that some of them (Catherine's hair and Peter's messy pocket) were not what I would consider aesthetic, at least not from some traditional point of view. The contrast between their work and my blue-grey-tin art work made me realize that I had been driven by the desire to create a piece of art, which would be beautiful. Yet, the experience it referred to was anything but beautiful. I sensed that the critical potential and significance of my distressing experience was somehow lost in the aesthetics of the art work. I also felt frustrated by my lack of understanding of the "language of the visual," particularly when compared to the "language of the written or said." I found difficulty not only in expressing myself visually but also in being able to recognize whether my experience could be read from the art work or not. To give an example, I intended to paint a grey foundation to make the canvas look oppressive, and to use silver tin to suggest a cold, impersonal atmosphere. The results were, to my surprise, quite different. The grey became more like a blue, and the silver tin glittered, so that it looked more like an attractive decoration than the alien, unwelcoming second skin of the conference room. The same happened to the red horse, who was supposed to be staring dangerously at the viewer, but the red and yellow colors of his eyes made him look more like a cheery decoration.

Perhaps no special skill would have been needed if I had realized that in visual art one can "find ways to articulate what [one] could not say but felt" (Camden Pratt, 2007: 253). I recognize now that my art work is quite an accurate representation of the second skin of the conference room, but not of the ways I had been affected by it. "Art work set us in the midst of knowings that are not tellable, but those knowings are 'sense-able' (Ellsworth, 2005: 162). My art work refers to the words I used to construe the second skin in the collective biography story. In this respect, it is a visual representation of a fully articulated and documented experience. Nevertheless, there are other things to say about the events in the conference room which I did not, or could not, say in the written story made public and read aloud to my colleagues. These burdensome and abjected feelings could have been expressed in my art work, if only I had abandoned the desire to control the process of its making; the desire, to which I clung so tenaciously.

> "Like an experience of the learning self, aesthetic experience holds the potential for the coming of a knowing, available only through acknowledgement and inaccessible through explanation. Explanation is simply unable to bear the weight of the 'knowings' that are aesthetic experience or the experience of the learning self. Explanation's failures in these realms are of huge consequence for both art and pedagogy." (Ellsworth, 2005: 162)

I wonder about the effects of writing about the visual. After I began to put in writing these reflections, the relationship to my blue-grey-tin art work has changed. While I was trying to explain its meaning and the process of its creation to the reader and also to myself, I began to understand it and to like it again. It is perhaps because the visual must be sometimes, or for some people, translated into words to be recognized as precious. When attending a visual art exhibition, I always look for the explanations of what the art work, with all its particular colors and forms, is supposed to signify. I need to know what can be said or written or thought about the visual to fully appreciate it and be affected by it. Paradoxically, while engaged in creating my piece of art, I was subjected by the same discourses of reason, planning and control, which my art work was supposed to critique. To write these reflections enabled me, on the contrary, to loosen the grip of the rationalist discourse and to envision different possibilities of becoming a creative subject; the subject open to dialogue with others, be they human or nonhuman, and to transformations such dialogue encourages.

> "It is an idea of dialogue not as an exchange but as a process of transformation where you lose

> absolutely the possibility of controlling the final result. And it goes to infinity, it goes to the universe, you get lost. And for human beings nowadays, and for women particularly, to get lost is a possibility and a risk, you know?" (Rinaldi, 2006: 184)

Susanne's account

Rather than extending the place stories, my experience of the art workshop was that it helped me to become more expansive in my telling of the story I discussed in Chapter Four of my first year as a young teacher working in an Aboriginal school.[i] What the art workshop did was bring me back into the story in quite a different way. It enabled me to create a parallel story—one that was not as propelled by the temporality of narrative.

I had brought in photographs from that time, on the other side of the country when I was very young. I had also brought in four pages of thin yellowed paper, typed more than twenty years ago with class lists of names and places, headed: "Where they come from." These gave me quite a shaky start. I was constrained by the literal qualities of the real names and faces, including myself then, in these artifacts. I could have written detailed descriptions of many of these kids and episodes I remembered from when I was there with them. I had already begun to do this in the story I had written at Bombo. But I didn't want to do more of this sort of analysis. Until now, I had never written about that time. Yet it had a profound effect and shaped me as a teacher (and a person) in ways that have never been easy to articulate. The physicality of these memories astounds me—children leaning on me, touching me, dark brown skin against skin, suddenly made irrevocably white in this place. What the story in Chapter Four told was my separation from, and difference from these kids. That story inscribed a series of binaries which kept us apart: they are students, I am teacher; they are black, I am white; they speak language, I speak English; they sit, I stand; they have trachoma and nits, I do not.

What the photos tell me is how we were together. Many of them have my earlier self in the middle of groups of children sitting around in different locations in the school. Others are of wall displays in the "Language" classroom where I worked alongside a Christian Brother monk and an Aboriginal teaching aide from one of the communities from which the children come. In the art workshop I look over the yellowed list I had forgotten I still had. The work I do with these traces of the past in the space of the art workshop helps me to be in two places at once, to take up two positions at the same time. In the story I have told in Chapter Four, I have taken myself up as "she," though in my talk here and there around the story, I write in the first person as "I." Through the further work I do in the art workshop, my work with the images, the slippage between "me" and "she" that erupts through my language no longer seems aberrant, but inevitable and even natural.

In the art workshop I begin to be loosened from the literal truth of the photographic image, and of memory as veridical truth, when I start to mask the image rather than to elaborate upon it. I blow up each of the photos on a color copier. One of them is of a cave painting from the inland Kimberley. I ignore the two ancestral Wandjina figures that were the main subject of the photograph and instead wrap and glue the other half of the image across a small canvas. This is the background to the photo, the wall of the cave. It is covered with paint, layers and layers of ochres of different shades. I can just see the outlines of hands, and a small white ghost image amongst all the fragments of other colors. I paint over it, dab by dab, with a small brush, my new teachers Alicia and Jade showing me how to mix the colors that I need. When the wall—itself already layers and layers of other people's loving labor over centuries—is entirely covered over by my own work, in shades that ghost what is underneath, I glue on a tiny cut-out image of myself sitting in the bottom left hand corner. In the original photograph this figure was sitting amongst a group of students, looking relaxed and completely immersed in the experience of being there, and in the cluster of bodies that surrounded her. They too are ghosts in the new image. The teacher's body still inclines towards them. She is still smiling at something one of them has said.

In the top right hand corner I draw a fish freehand in ink with a fine black pen copying it closely from one of the posters from the Language classroom. The photograph shows that the pinboards that surround the classroom have been divided by strips of paper into panels for each language group. Each panel carries small posters of words and images drawn by students. This fish comes from the Kija language, from Turkey

Creek (now called Warmun community). The name of the fish in that language is "kuntaril." The long sweep down to his eyes and mouth suggest that he might be a freshwater barramundi—she caught them too when she lived there—but now I am not so sure and I cannot draw as accurately as the children. I copy this carefully from the poster in the photo and seal it all over with shellac which gives it a golden glow.

In this work the young teacher is part of the place, rather than separate from it. She was part of an endeavor to bring what these kids knew into the classroom and to value it. The subtlety of this image provides me with a new means of generalizing about that experience of being there—one that does not flatten out the detail but foregrounds one or two specific elements to represent it. The fish—kuntaril—operates as a sort of metonym. I draw the fish because he is the most identifiable poster on the wall but he says something more as well about the young woman who finds herself there. Most crudely she might be a fish out of water in some ways but she is also immersed. The strangeness on my tongue now of kuntaril, reminds me that my place there was earned partly by my knowledge of language then. I had recently completed studies in Aboriginal linguistics in the final year of my undergraduate degree. The young woman in the image was not immune to the magic of language and this extraordinary place. In the art work I created, she is also part of the wall of the cave, with the white ghost haunting the underlayers of paint and shellac.

The second art work I did, I lost straight after the workshop, dropped on a path or in the car park. But it was important as a bridge from one piece to the next. I spent a long time cutting out letters with a blade to try and make a stencil of the lists of place names. They were too many and too long and I realized I did not have the time and that I was still—again—too literal. But now I had begun to work with the places and their names. I painted a white canvas with white paint and set it aside. Though the list of "Where they come from" was like a mantra, or a song, I didn't yet know what to do with it. I went back to the bodies who still jostled against my skin in my memory. Now I remembered the girls that I taught more than the boys who had crowded in to my first story. I cut out the sitting silhouettes of three of the girls I remembered most vividly and—with Alicia's help—screen-printed them on to a strip of brown silk that Bronwyn had brought. I used another shade of brown, more ochre like. They looked so at ease in their bodies, in their loose limbs and open knees. More at ease in their posture and their flesh than many women I have known, than myself. At the top I stenciled: "Where they come from:" and underneath, freehand with the black ink pen, I wrote in all the names of the places, all in lower case and butting against each other, a long string of letters that reformed as you looked at them into words: "broomegibbriverstationhallscreekwyndham...." I put a dot at the end of my list of place names and started listing the names of languages I remembered in the same style. This time the words were not English words laid over aboriginal country but words from Aboriginal languages with sounds and combinations that are alien to English: "kijanyangumartabardibidyadanga." I began with such a rush of joy as if this was what I knew, what I wanted to say about how special the new knowledge that I glimpsed there, about ways of being in the world, was to me. But I faltered at Bardi—an extra stroke had accidentally turned it into Bandi and I felt undone. I remembered, as well, after my hand had already written out the word, that Bidyadanga was the Aboriginal name for La Grange Mission and not a language group. I remembered how far I was now from where I had been then, how much I had forgotten, how much I didn't know. I only lived there for three years and only worked at the school for two years. I was never as deeply involved with the school or the children as those staff who were practicing Catholics, and so much of school life turned on religious rituals about which I was ambivalent as an ex-Catholic. On a website documenting the history of the school I find that I am not mentioned at all. So perhaps my absence haunts that history too, like the experience haunts me. The arts practice led me to a way of working with my memories that was, simultaneously, about masking and revealing.

Peter's account

I had thought, in advance of this writing that I am doing now, of what I might say, of how I might begin, but decided against actually beginning until I had read what others had written. So here I am, writing and responding at the same time, taking up the words "translating," "lost" and "wax" that I already find in the text, and using them as my own (as I had planned to do anyway). I am interested in the movement between speech, writing and the visual; talk, text and art; and specifically the acts of translation that are employed in these movements. How does one thing become another, and what happens in the process of that becoming? I remember, as I write this, that the talking, the writing, the art making, and this writing about the art making, were emergent from biographical stories; from recollections of lived experience. So, when I am talking about movements and translations, of one thing becoming another, I think, as I write, about myself, about anybody, and the formative conditions and occasions through which we might too become something other; be transformed ourselves in the acts of translation that we make. Do you notice the slippage in my sentences between speech and writing, between remembering and representation, between the inanimate and the animate, between myself and another? These are the movements I wish to trace. I am as much interested in these movements and acts of creation as I am in the acts of painting, printing, stitching and making that I performed on that day in the art class.

> "Creativity is not just the quality of thinking of each individual but is also an interactive, relational and social project. It requires a context that allows it to exist, to be expressed, to become visible."
> (Rinaldi, 2006: 119-20)

My question then, is not only about those acts of translation that might make these movements possible, but about what might be lost in the process, of the sense there might be of something slipping away from us. What, Bronwyn asks, might be partially lost, hidden and revealed? How, Katerina asks, might the language of the written/said become the language of the visual? And Susanne provokes us to think of the movement between a veridical truth and an iteration of it in which detail is masked rather than elaborated. So, back to my words, the words I have chosen to shape this account of my day in the art class: "translation," "lost," "wax".

When I was an adolescent, I was fascinated by the Art Nouveau movement of art and design. I was particularly drawn to its sinuous, sensuous, organic forms. I loved the work of the French glass-makers, and of Rene Lalique in particular. Why am I telling you this? My reflections on the art class, on this question of translation and loss evoked a memory of a particular technique used by Lalique: cire perdue, or lost wax. In this technique forms were modeled from wax and then encased in a ceramic paste. After the paste hardened, the paste-covered model was heated to melt out the wax model, leaving a hollow ceramic mold into which molten glass was poured. When the glass had hardened, the mold was broken away, revealing the glass object inside. Only one model could be made of any object, and that model was destroyed in the melting of the wax. I tell you about this because I think of it as an example of the extent to which acts of translation, of movement from one thing or form to another, involves a constitutive loss: something is lost in order that something be made. Further, that which is made cannot be the same as that from which it was made: something is lost in translation; emergent from transformation. Perhaps, as Susanne suggests, this is a haunting absence; an absence that haunts the present.

So, how might a moment become a memory; a memory become an oral account; an oral account become a written account; a written account become a visual account? And what acts of translation, transformation and representation, of loss and emergence might be involved in these movements?

To the art class: faced with the daunting task of beginning, of not knowing where or how to begin, I began a number of things at the same time. A painted board; tracings of words from my written account onto tissue paper; cut-up fragments of text; screen printing, stitching; a mixture of familiar and newly acquired media and skills. I didn't know what I was doing, where I was headed, or what might ever become of the fragments I was creating. All I was certain of was that the idea of loss, of shedding, peeling, becoming raw and starting over was the element from my biographical memory story that I was working with (an account of the ending of a ten-year relationship and the selling of my home and its contents). The art making felt rather chaotic and messy, and I suppose, now I think about it, that was pretty much how the experience of ending my relationship felt all those years ago. Perhaps something of that experience had bled into the making of the art that was a remembrance of it. The writing of the story, however, the act of writing, was much more neatly crafted. It was shaped by an aesthetic dedication to the text, to the desire to craft something spare and elegant.

And yet my art making was chaotic and messy; far from elegant. It was a messy assemblage of the fragments I had created, and the final effect was of something more ugly and disordered than spare and elegant. This messiness was at once satisfying—as a representation or translation of the memory—and repulsive—as something that did not conform to my idea of aesthetics. Before the workshop, what I had vaguely imagined I might make, was something colorful, vibrant, luscious, elegant and sophisticated—and not the black and white thing slashed with red that I had created.

> "The essence of Being is the shock of the instant [*le coup*]. Each time, 'Being' is always an instance [*un coup*] of Being (a lash, blow, beating, shock, knock, an encounter, an access). As a result, it is also always an instance of with: *singulars singularly together...*" (Nancy, 2000: 33).

This difference between what I had imagined and what I had done (and perhaps who I was and who I had become) was as much shaped by my limits as by my desire to capture the messiness of the memory. By this I mean that I didn't actually have the skill to make something as beautiful as anything I might imagine; that there was an act of translation that would fall short between my imagination and my capacity to realize that which I had imagined. A desire to reproduce with veracity what I had imagined, and a recognition of the impossibility of doing so. And so I worked with what I knew I was able to do: to work with the constitutive messiness of experience in order to produce something that was more truthful in its messiness that its imagined beauty.

I seem to be suggesting that ignorance, inexperience and messiness may perhaps produce a verisimilitude that otherwise haunts our more competent and confident accounts of ourselves, and that it is through the disruption of our familiar practices of writing, through the unfamiliar practices of art making, that we might have been enabled to translate and transform our experience from something more than a recollection of the past, into something more like a reinvigoration of the present. What might this say about pedagogy as a possible movement, as a moment in which the movement of the subject from one thing, one state, one body to another might be accomplished? This movement, as I imagine it, does not fetishize mastery, agency and certainty, but rather, embraces the messiness of knowing, experiencing, being and doing. It also understands that what is lost in this movement might be the genesis for that which it might be possible to find. And who knows, until we lose ourselves, what there might be to find, what movements it might be possible to follow and what possible moments, what moments of possibility, might await us.

Catherine's account

I take up Peter's suggestions of a pedagogy that embraces "the messiness of knowing, experiencing, being and doing." Messiness I know intimately. She inhabits my underworld soul. Although she is hidden and unwelcome in academia, a place of "certainty, agency and mastery," she breathes life and understanding into all that I do there (Camden Pratt, 2002, 2006, 2007, 2008). There in the pedagogical and research spaces I inhabit, she is my ally. A sometimes irascible ally but dependable when I meet her with respect for her wisdom; don't hurry her, don't foreclose and attempt to neaten her. Messiness and art making cannot be separated (cf. Chapter Three). Making art takes me into the underworld where I journey until I emerge back into the upper world with new knowledges, just as the mythical Persephone and Isis emerged from their long underworld sojourns. Left to my own devices in my studio at home I cannot determine how long I will journey or how deep I will go or what will emerge. The process is more important than the final piece I make, although the piece will hold for me all the layers of my journey towards its completion. And it may take weeks, months or years to complete. It may be complete for a time and then call me back to journey with it again. But in this instance, I'd been invited to spend a day art making, extending place pedagogy stories into visual art.

In the weeks before our working together I wondered how my underworld soul and I would meet as I worked in the academic art-making classroom with my research colleagues. I felt my soul tighten against expectations of a product. Whose expectations? I tighten against fears of being seen, of my messiness displayed naked and vulnerable, of a possible refusal of creative emergence under such conditions of making art in a collegial community. And now I'm invited to write about the art making. Beginning to write I resist this tidying as I always do; this interpreting of the messiness into something with boundaries and seeming certainties, to become acceptable, legitimate in the academic domain in which the verbal linear remains privileged. I respect the mystery in art making, its alchemical wisdom. Mapping the territories of our art making and place pedagogies requires this respect, this knowing that we cannot fix the alchemy of our engagements and their specificities.

And so I continue to write, welcoming a narrative text and being willing to reflect aspects of the messy chaotic world I enter in making art.

The story I was interested in exploring further occurred in my clowning class discussed in Chapter Five. I was unsure of what materials to take with me. I decided to take my old fashioned brown vinyl "beauty case" that held my clowning bits and pieces including my worn out faded pink satin *pointe* shoes, red plastic clown nose, sheet music of "somewhere over the rainbow" and my long golden hair which I had cut off as a seventeen-year-old and kept wrapped up in newspaper inside the beauty case. As an afterthought, I took a photocopy of my mother's published writings as a seventeen-year old which she had pasted into a black-covered exercise book which she titled her "cuttings book." I also included her old faded-brown exercise book filled with recipe ideas, shopping lists and ideas for short stories written in shorthand—the script stenographers used—when she was a mother with five children and me on the way. All these I placed into the beauty case. My hand was turning the front door knob to leave for the day feeling somewhat hurried and unprepared when I turned back into the house and took a dried pomegranate fruit from above my desk. As I put it into my bag I saw the small round black and white ceramic plate imaged with a woman's skeleton form dismembered yet whole, a skull embedded in the design. I had bought this in Mexico City in the central plaza on *El Dia de los Muertos* (The Day of the Dead Festival) in 2004. Then I had been on my way home from visiting Frida Kahlo's Blue House in Mexico City en route from a conference in Cuba on Social Justice Pedagogies. Now I took it, placed it carefully into the beauty case, and hurried out the door.

...I want to write the in-betweens of these lines, these descriptions of acts in words that cannot cast a shadow in their flattened text. The unraveling begins but I pull back. I am neatening the messy in order to tell the linear story here of my art making that day. How can I show you here the multi-layers that leap out to me as I write as I re-member the day's art making? I wonder at its genesis, my heart skips in excitement with the connections I am making I breathe in and out and return to the linear text knowing that to unravel into that messiness here is to risk losing sense in the text and I wonder if I am ready for that...

At the time, I was puzzled and a little uncomfortable at what I brought with me that day. Macabre. Lacking luster or freshness. And why bring my mother's writings—what was that about? My discomfort increased as we began a show and tell and I saw what the others had brought to work with. I felt the ominous rattling of my underworld and told myself not to worry about a product, not to expect myself to complete an "art work," just to pay attention and live into the process and its intelligence. Bronwyn's generous offer of our choosing from her rich fabrics grounded me in the collective nature of our work; Katerina's and my time together, exploring the limits of the UWS photocopier, re-established our emergent collegial bond; Jade and Alicia's wealth of delicious art supplies and their warm explanations of what they could offer us excited me and I began to feel safer to pay attention and express what may come in my art making. While I have made and exhibited art over the last ten years in response to research questions (Camden Pratt, 2003, 2007), I have no training. I was conscious that my colleagues may see me as "expert" or at the very least "competent" and I felt a performance anxiety—a downside of collaborative work in a process context.

My previous work (Camden Pratt, 2002, 2003, 2007) has used mixed media and so I set about exploring the materials I had brought and their potential qualities and applications in opening up the story of my clowning class. I like to have lots of things around me before I begin; I may not use them all but I like the free range of my ideas being triggered by the materials themselves. I realized I did not want to use the objects themselves as mixed media pieces and decided instead to photocopy each object. Bronwyn had brought in a few quotes from Ceppi and Zini and I chose one, "The environment generates a sort of psychic skin, an energy giving second skin made of writings, images, materials, objects, and colors, which reveals the presence of the children even in their absence" (Ceppi and Zini, 1998: 17). Not knowing how come I chose it, but trusting the intelligence in the process I photocopied it too. All my photocopying meant I ended up with lots of black and white, which gave me a sense of the always photo-imaged nature of the memory of events. Memory immediately shifts the actual event into an imaged event and in doing so changes its shades and tones, can blur its outlines and fade its shape over multiple re-memberings.

I found an old piece of cardboard box from the stack that the students, who regularly used this art room, used as palettes and took it to my table. This was my initial canvas. I stood a long time simply looking at the old piece of cardboard, its creases and tears, the places where the corrugated insides were revealed through its torn surface. This is what I wanted to show. This is what was revealed though my clowning class. My corrugated insides revealed as the smooth surface layers of myself were torn aside. No longer boxed; no longer useful as a demarcated container.

The "Becoming Blossom" story had clear stages—Jade suggested a triptych and so I searched for more cardboard pieces. I stood a long time surveying my three pieces of cardboard, all different, all the same, conscious that around me each of my colleagues was deeply engaged in their work. I was close to Bronwyn and watched every now and then as she worked with her fabrics, enjoying their fluidity, their colors, her amazement at her creation. I worked with one canvas and began to highlight the corrugations, painting red splashes. Cutting up my *Dia de los Muertos* photocopy, I placed the dismembered pieces in a corner, their wholeness in separation magnified. I wanted layers, I wanted revelations, I wanted transparency, translucency, I wanted, I wanted, I wanted. Rattle, rattle...try some of the wax I thought, that could work...but it didn't—too much wax dulled the canvas, didn't satisfy whatever it was in me that was irritated, hungry. I found some transparent paper, rectangular like my canvas and laid it over the canvas. Some of the wet red paint stuck to it as I pulled it off the canvas dissatisfied with its layering effect. What was I resisting? What could I not hear? What perhaps didn't I want to hear?

I laughed to myself. There she was all the time. My mother—her madness. How come I had not seen it, seen her? No wonder my underworld rattled! Making art about place pedagogy, opening up and exploring the inter-relationships between place and pedagogy meant opening the physical place in which I had taken the clowning class. I am surprised by this opening up and yet I wonder how I had not seen it before and its relationship to the weeks during which I stood wearing my clown mask unable to do anything but cry.

> "—beginning from the one, or from the other,
> —beginning from their togetherness, understood now as the One, now as the Other,
> —but thinking, absolutely and without reserve, beginning from the 'with' *as the proper essence of the one whose Being is nothing other than with-one-another* [*l'un-avec-l'autre*]." (Nancy, 2000: 34)

Yes, its awareness had lapped at my edges, but I was young then—thirty-three—not yet fully aware of my mother's influences on my life. When I was a baby/child/teenager/adult, my mother spent most of her life living in psychiatric institutions—one of which was the place I had written about in my clown story. It was here that I spent two years in drama training. I stood silent looking at my art work struggling with this interruption of my mother yet again into my art making, into my research (Camden Pratt, 2002, 2006, 2007). Peter was nearby and so I whispered to him something like, "Ugh, god I hate this—there's my life again!" I didn't want this here in this group researching this new area! I felt shame rise up again familiar even after so many years of researching and writing about legacies of maternal madness. Peter laughed, said something like "It's always autobiographical—we can't escape our stories." I smiled at him—or was it a grimace—and entered into my art making now saying "Yes" to the reverberations of my mother's madness that echoed in the walls of the hall in which I'd found my clown.

The long white screen printing paper lay on the table and I decided to go with this as a canvas, giving up my cardboard, letting go of what I'd already spent time on. I carefully pulled some skeins of my long blonde hair from the parcel I'd brought and glued it onto the new canvas—this gave me great satisfaction though I didn't know why. Next I glued a photocopy of the title page of my mother's cuttings book left of centre along the side of my canvas, her fine spidery handwriting neatly proclaiming her publishing successes and dated 1929. This is my talisman—the evidence of the mother I never knew, her luminous talent as a young writer shining off the page. I place a photocopy of the dismembered yet intact *Dia de los Muertos* bottom right, covering it with a waxed transparent sheet which I later sewed into place. Now I am willing to go where it leads me, I am driven-led by a hidden process, making aesthetic decisions as I go based on my inner satisfaction in response to the outer representations on the canvas (Camden Pratt, 2007). I stand back and ask myself what is going on here on this canvas? What space has been opened up in and through this pedagogical moment? Where does place pedagogy theory fit in here? Then I see it as if I had not seen it before and smile again at the sub-conscious intelligence that drives an art making process long before the conscious wakes up to it. Of course, the quote Bronwyn brought with her. Now I re-read it and cut out the word "children" and insert instead my own words now italicized, I play with re-presentations and meanings: "The environment generates a sort of psychic skin, an energy giving second skin made of writings, images, materials, objects, and colors, which reveals the presence of the (m)other even in (t)he(i)r absence" (Ceppi and Zini, 1998: n.p.).

I place the quote on brown paper using thin metal and an engraving iron to inscribe the word "mother." I have watched Katerina use this technique and like its effect, the way in which the engraving goes into the metal breaking its skin, the way in which it cannot be rubbed out. I reflect on the unknown mothers who shared this particular psychiatric hospital—Callan Park/Broughton Hall/Rozelle—concurrently with my mother and over the many years of its use since 1885. I note the links between women's social history and the history of "madness" and cut out the letters of the word "their" so that I can move them to reveal the "her" in "their."

Ah, I breathe out in satisfaction with how theorizing from the personal makes a spaciousness as the personal becomes political, moving from isolation to inclusion. Bronwyn comes across to my table and says "You might like this" and hands me a small handmade square of paper, its centre square a curious silver that turns golden in certain lights, the square's surrounds a parchment color. It's just right for the top left hand corner—again I do not know why, but it satisfies me and the art work is complete. I know there are other things to do to complete a series. However, this one is done.

On and off through the process, I take time out to walk around the art room, looking at my colleagues' work, marveling at our creative processes, our differences, our delights and challenges—I am in awe at this process. Always the messiness co-habiting, co-located, the materials and our processes, the chaos. I marvel at Bronwyn's layered garment, at Peter's packaged work, Katerina's Foucault, inscribed and re-inscribed, Sue's rich glowing desert reds and browns, her students present in their Aboriginal languages, her youthful face so open so eager so white—her excitement and amazement at what she'd created. Alicia and Jade moving among us, quiet, encouraging, suggesting.

My work is plain, black and white with some splashes of red paint coming through from behind. I like this. It contrasts with the work I have done before in which color played a central role. I laugh to myself—I cannot escape the red paint, the wet multi-storied viscosity of women's blood which is central in my previous art works (Camden Pratt, 2002, 2007). When we talk about our art work in the classroom I resist a verbal fixed storying of my work, knowing its revelations continue as I live with it. Yet we are asked to tell its story, its revelations. I know that I can only tell a partial story, only what I can see now and articulate back into words from a wordless, imaged process. I talk about how my art work stories the underworld, *El Dia de los Muertos*—The Day of the Dead—when the living honor their ancestors with rituals and gifts. About how although the second skin of Rozelle Hospital itself is not represented as such on my art work, it continues its psychic presence. It holds my clowning class which is in the impulse for and subject of the art work. It is present in my mother as she speaks her poetic self through her 'cuttings book' and onto my art work—a self later destroyed by years of madness and its psychiatric treatments. I am puzzled about my hair and its significance in my art work—just as I was puzzled all those years ago when I had brought it to subsequent clowning class as a prop. When Katerina comments on the dangerous quality the hair gives the work, I am surprised and despite feeling somewhat embarrassed I have no reason to offer for its inclusion. Yet as I write now I realize that when I cut off my long hair after an illness that brought me close to death, I was a teenager and the same age as my mother when she began her cuttings book. What does this mean? I'm not sure, simply that there is this parallel. What else the use of my hair signifies I am not sure or rather I meet my messiness again...There are layers here of her-storical family stories which I resist telling but which sit with me as I write; as I silence as I reveal/don't reveal. Their complexities pull at me demanding to be heard to be made sense of; to find their place in this telling; in this reverberation of my mother's life in mine. My her-storical context when I cut off my hair eddies around me, its griefs helped fill the pool of tears I could not contain as I stood with my clown mask trying to find my clown. It is a messiness too big for this telling in this place, this neatened collaborative text...

As I write I wonder about Frida Kahlo's art, the place of her hair in her life and paintings—particularly her 1940 Self-Portrait with Cropped Hair (Herrera, 1983:opp 290), her fascination with *El Dia de los Muertos*, how she has mothered me as an artist and woman through her art work and life. I begin to wonder about the second skin of the various mothers that are revealed in my art work. Staying with this, I look at the piece of paper from Bronwyn and reflect on the ways in which I may have located her as mother in my emerging academic journey. It is through her strong encouragement I published from my PhD, that I continue this fraught academic journey in which I struggle to find my place and way of doing academia. I wonder about the clear place of this piece of paper on my art work—not photocopied, not over-layered, not changed, simply placed as if a counterpoint to the other second skins. I did not reveal all this as we talked in the classroom that day, my messiness confronted me, I could not speak all of what I saw. Then as now, I felt pleased with my creation, pleased at its plainness, its sparsity, its layers, its hidden/revealed stories.

Peter wrote of the possibilities of a pedagogy which embraces the "messiness of knowing, experiencing, being and doing" as enabling movements in possibility and of possibility. Art making with the focus on my clowning story opened up possibilities that were hidden in my verbal and written story in Chapter Five. This silenced story was revealed through and in messiness. Messiness continues to hold the story's holographic layers. My underworld ally resists totalizing the neatening of this telling, calling me to dig deeper into the new messiness that is revealed as layers rise to the upper-world aesthetically represented surface. I like knowing this. The alchemy remains intact.

And so...

So what was the second skin in this place of the workshop? Quiet voices, rich colors, Peter's laughter, Catherine's hair and her underworld, Sue's cave, Katerina's slivers of tin and wood on a grey-blue surface with Foucault looking on, Bronwyn's 'skirt' and Peter's packet of hidden words and peeling skin and his smiling face blocked out. The objects that we worked with, that worked on us and with us, included the paint, the boards and the machines made available in the classroom, as well as the highly personal materials we had each chosen to bring with us. These objects were, in a sense the not-yet-formed second skin that we were working on. The quiet, attentive presence of our teachers, Jade and Alicia, responsive to our work, quietly saving us from disaster, and giving us courage to keep going in the face of our lack of skill or courage, were our Jo (Chapter Two) and our Bridget (Chapter Five), creating, with their strategy of attention, a safe space where we could experiment, move into the chaos of the not-yet-known, and find a truth of ourselves and of the not-yet-understood idea we wanted to express. They made us strong enough to work through our fears and insecurities—our lack of knowledge and competencies. Their quiet presence created that safe plot of land that we each needed in order to launch out in our singular lines of flight with all our incompetencies and fears available for anyone to see. We were a group of students together engaged in a collaborative moment of deeply personal differenciation. In letting go of the requirement that we think in rational, articulate lines, we were able to open ourselves up to the unexpected, the chaotic, the painful and yet simultaneously joyous experimentation that art affords. The collective we created enabled an intense and safe in-turning, a focused attention to the particular folds of being we'd chosen to work with, allowing us to move from solitude to community and back throughout the day. The room itself provided a second skin full of light and rich resources to work with in a permission giving way, with enough space to move between solitude and awareness of and openness to the others.

This chapter, written by all who were present at the Bombo workshop, brings to culmination the collective exploration of pedagogical encounters that began at Bombo in a white house with a view of the sea where we spent a week recalling and exploring our lived experiences of spaces of learning, and later, a week together going over these chapters together, weaving in the threads of other memories, other spaces we have been in, into this rethinking of pedagogy and place. In this next chapter, subtitled "the architecture of pedagogical encounters," we draw attention to the physicality of learning spaces through an examination of the tertiary sites we have learned and taught in.

Notes

[i] See Gannon (2008) for the images and an expanded account of this workshop.

7
SECOND SKIN: THE ARCHITECTURE OF PEDAGOGICAL ENCOUNTERS
BRONWYN DAVIES, CATHERINE CAMDEN PRATT, CONSTANCE ELLWOOD, SUSANNE GANNON, KATERINA ZABRODSKA AND PETER BANSEL

Lyotard wrote in *The Postmodern Condition: A Report on Knowledge* that, sociologically speaking:

> A *self* does not amount to much, but no self is an island; each exists in a fabric of relations that is now more complex and mobile than ever before. Young or old, man or woman, rich or poor, a person is always located at "nodal points" of specific communication circuits, however tiny these may be. Or better: one is always located at a post through which various kinds of messages pass. No one, not even the least privileged among us, is ever entirely powerless over the messages that traverse and position him at the post of sender, addressee, or referent. (Lyotard, 1979/84: 8)

This existence of the individual self or subject as a nodal point in networks of communication circuits was central to the discursive turn in the late 1970s and 1980s, a turn that shifted, fundamentally the way we understood what it meant to be human. Human subjects were no longer understood as the sovereign agents of liberalism, but as interconnected and interdependent, subjected through discourse and becoming active subjects through discourse. No longer existing outside the flows of communication that make them up, they are yet still able to take action, to have agency, to change the line of action or even the fabric of relations in which they are, with others, embedded.

Building on that shift, the spatial turn that we have explored in this book, locates human existence in a network of sensory connections. Those networks extend beyond human and discursive networks to the animate and inanimate world: the "world itself is like a single 'skin' over which our senses, expelled and diffused, extend like networks" (Ceppi and Zini, 1998: n.p.). Architecture and things take on, in this spatial turn, much greater salience, becoming actors in the networks in which we are now, no longer nodal "posts," but ourselves networks spreading out into our surroundings, and our surroundings spreading themselves out into us.

The physical or material contexts in which we each take up our existence are thus brought to life in this spatial turn, given power, understood as having effects. The ways of thinking that are brought to bear in this spatial shift extend beyond sociology to include architecture, biology, music, art and psychology. The subject who is thought of as existing separate from these networks is impoverished. Wilson, for example, deconstructs the human/non-human binary, pointing out that we limit our evolutionary capacity if we accept human as the dominant term, or as beings separated from and superior to other ontological systems. She writes:

> Darwin's system of evolution specifies the ontological coimplication of animals, man, plants, rocks, and emotions. Each mode of materiality is built through its complicitous relations to others, and heredity is governed by a heterogeneous set of forces...By accentuating the structural intimacy of biology and psychology in The Expression of the Emotions in Man and Animals, Lorenz hints at one of the most underexamined aspects of Darwin's work: that evolution...is radically heterogeneous; certainly it is biological, but it is also psychological, cultural, geological, oceanic, and meteorological. (Wilson, 2004: 69)

Human existence in this understanding is not an existence that is separate from other forms of existence. Human, animal, earth and other matter—all exist, and exist in networks of relationality, dependence and influence. The spatial turn is thus also a material turn, beyond the discursive turn, that aims to provide "ways of understanding the agency, significance, and ongoing transformative power of the world—ways that account for the myriad 'intra-actions'...between phenomena that are material, discursive, human, more than human, corporeal and technological" (Alaimo and Hekman, 2008: 5). In this chapter we will focus on the relations between tertiary teachers and students and the physical/relational spaces—walls, doors, furniture, bodies, technologies—that make up what we have called the pedagogical encounter.

We borrow the term second skin from the Reggio Emilia context and use it to invoke all those elements of pedagogical space, the visible and invisible architectures of learning spaces at universities and their psychic effects. In Reggio Emilia inspired schools, documents that tell the story of children's artistic becomings are displayed on the walls of the hallways and classrooms, generating a second skin that becomes active. The ideal environment in a Reggio Emilia inspired school is:

SECOND SKIN: THE ARCHITECTURE OF PEDAGOGICAL ENCOUNTERS 133

> An environment that documents not only the results but also the processes of learning and knowledge-building, that narrate the didactic paths and state the values of reference. The environment generates a sort of psychic skin, an energy giving second skin made of writings, images, materials, objects, and colors, which reveals the presence of the children even in their absence. (Ceppi and Zini, 1998: n.p.)

The Reggio Emilia classroom is designed to facilitate relations with others and with place itself. It is embedded in the ongoing life of the community. In emphasizing the importance of relations between a classroom and its outside, the Reggio Emilia classroom brings us closer to the Deleuzian understanding of architecture, where the inner space of a building is not seen as different from its outside, but as a fold of the outside. In accord, Ceppi and Zini write about the

> ...strong relationship between the inside and outside of the school building. A school should be a place that 'senses' what is happening outside—from the weather to seasonal changes, from the time of day to the rhythms of the town—precisely because it exists in a specific place and time. (Ceppi and Zini, 1998: n.p.)

This place and time are integrally connected to the Deleuzian possibility of becoming—opening ourselves to difference in ourselves and in the other, the other being not just other human beings, but the physical objects, landscapes and other materialities with which and in which we take up our existence. In her discussion of Deleuze's thinking about architecture, Grosz conceptualizes buildings as texts, which "do things, make things, perform connections, bring about new alignments" (2001: 58). Classrooms are thus places which ideally should be open to their outside where outside is understood not only as an outer space but also, and more importantly, as what is different, unassimilable, and as yet unthought.

In our first story about experiencing a second skin the story-teller responds at the level of the heart to the inside-outside relationship enabled by the architecture of the inner city building in which she is studying. She begins her story as she is walking toward the building:

Bare road. Stained bitumen. Cars. Street signs. No parking. No standing. One way. Concrete. Colorless. This is the world as I approach.

I tap my seven-digit code into the entry pad and the wide glass doors slide open. I go in. I enter. The sunlight gleams in through the glass roof. The sky is blue beyond it. The polished woods and the glass floors of the upper levels glint and glow. But, above all, there is space, space lifting the building out through its own roof, space shooting upwards, carrying my heart with it.

The joy of the inner space arises in marked contrast to the heavy striations and prohibitions of the street outside. The inside space is smooth space connected to the sky and to a lifting heart. The second skin of her pedagogical space is elemental—marked by light and space and lift—even transcendent. Buchanan and Lambert analyze such spaces in terms of a Deleuzian unfolding: "The great architects, then, are those who can use immobile pieces to carry the eye off the horizon; who can grab hold of movement using static pincers and create a structure that is not 'frozen music', but an orchestral piece unfolding in infinitive time" (Buchanan and Lambert, 2005: 8). In this story, it seems that the architect's vision—attuned to light and sky and space—works in relation with the energies of the student; the space itself contributes to the creativity and optimism of the activities embarked upon within it. In contrast to the linearity and constraints of the outside streets in this story, it is within a university building that the openness of new thought—literally experienced as a multisensorial line of flight—becomes possible. "Architecture becomes pedagogical and pedagogy becomes architectural," and "their place of joining creates a membrane where the brain/mind/body and the 'outside world' touch and interpenetrate, flow into and interfuse each other" (Ellsworth, 2005: 48).

In many university settings, however, the walls are often blank, dirty, deserted. Notice boards, student advertisements, labels on doors, occasional photos from successful workshops or conference posters are like islands in the sea of accumulated dust and drabness. Corridors are typified by blankness and silence or by the noise of busy bodies jostling against each other on their way to somewhere else. Occasionally they are adorned by works of art generated outside the academy and locked in safe glass boxes or otherwise secured against theft—thus generating a gap between the valued work of art and the untrustworthy viewer. The second skin of a learning place can be energy-giving or energy-sapping. The walls and windows, the ceilings and corners, the interactive and relational possibilities they make possible may damp us down, suck away our energy, or fire us up, enabling new connections and understandings. They may invite us into serene openings, into new thought and new relations with others similarly engaged in learning.

In relation to these stories of our own teaching places we ask, along with Ceppi and Zini (1998: n.p.), what is the difference between "a serene, amiable livable place," and a place that fails as an "educational context." Livable places, they suggest, recognize the importance of the senses: "Neurobiological research has clearly demonstrated the co-protagonism of the senses in the construction and processing of knowledge and individual and group memory. It follows that an unstimulating environment tends to dull and deafen our perceptions" (Ceppi and Zini: 1998: n.p.). A learning space that follows Reggio Emilia principles is multisensory "not so much in the sense of being simply rich in stimuli but having different sensory values so that each individual can tune into his or her own personal reception characteristics" (Ceppi and Zini, 1998: n.p.). An unstimulating classroom is a place where no energy is generated. The alchemy of new ideas that may have seemed possible outside the room, may not survive the room itself.

The second of our stories describes a university classroom where the dullness of the room carries over into the relations within it, which are also dull, and even hostile. The story holds the teacher's moment of entry into the classroom:

Everything in it is the same no-color as every other university classroom. It has the same permanently stained whiteboard. Concealing what might be a bright blue day, it has the same no-color regulation blinds, in the same jagged, unloved state. There are too many chairs for the space, impeding movement and establishing uncomfortable relationships. The students line up, their backs to the back wall, their eyes dulled or accusing. Crossing the threshold into the room is like dropping below zero, the brain numbs, and new ideas are forgotten as the mind freezes over.

We have seen this room everywhere, in chronically under-funded schools and universities. They are places where nothing new seems possible: "a divisible homogenous space striated in all directions" (Deleuze and Guattari, 1987: 223). Rooms such as this within schools and universities can carry the burden of the neoliberal order with its regulations, its cost cutting and its mass organizational practices. The "striated" space of an-other alien matter grows over and into one's own. The over-coded striations take hold of memory and imagination seeming to leave no space for the emergent possibility of new ideas, of movement and of becoming. The lines of flight that Deleuze and Guattari envisage as enabling new thought and the circulation of desire and imagination are unimaginable in such places.

The narrator in this story sees the colorless, uncared-for room with its regulation fittings and feels her own loss of capacity to think and to relate to the students. The walls narrate blandness, the blankness of no-thought, the surly resentment; they shut out the day. Through her eyes the students become like the walls, dull and lifeless. Striated in lines of power that require obedience and consent to powerlessness (Davies, 2008), the students mimic the walls and the walls mimic them. Far from Deleuze's idea of becoming as "pure movement" in which there is a blending "into the wall but the wall has become alive" (Deleuze and Parnet, 2002: 127), to enter the classroom—to cross that "threshold"—is to abandon the possibility of movement and thus of effective learning and teaching. The teacher's sensory memory of this space moves beyond the visual. It is carried through the atmosphere created in the room which is bleak and chill and permeates her body and her mind, making her feel as blank and as numb as the walls themselves. The new ideas generated elsewhere, the life of ideas, cannot make it over the threshold.

Our third story holds the same bleakness. It takes us to a conference where the narrator, also a young academic, was to co-present a workshop on an innovative methodology that she was introducing into her discipline. Although the audience still hopes to learn from her and her co-presenter, she reads the room as actively damping down her capacity for new thought, and as marking the new methodology she wants to talk about as marginal.

I am standing in front of lines of chairs in a computer room, which is filling with people. The room is in an old, ugly high school building and I am just about to give my opening speech at a workshop I have organized with my friend, who's sitting in front of me. The walls of the room are entirely covered with posters from the conference, none of which relate to the theme of the workshop. Around the whole room are tables with computers on them. I feel strangely disconnected from this place. I am already intensely aware of the fact that both the place and the atmosphere in the room are adverse to the collaborative and informal meeting I've had in my mind while preparing and desiring the workshop. There are many more people than I have expected and they are looking at me with anticipation. I would like to move the tables, or myself, so that I won't be directly facing the rows of people, but it is not possible. On the chairs closer to me sit my friends, and students I've been

SECOND SKIN: THE ARCHITECTURE OF PEDAGOGICAL ENCOUNTERS   137

teaching. I feel responsible to them and obliged to perform an engaging opening. In the first line of chairs, I can see my boyfriend, who was not supposed to be here. The rest of the room is crowded with people I do not know, some of them are said to be experts in their fields. Some people sit in the aisles and some just next to the door, far from me, as in a shadow. I know that this is the moment when I should really start to speak but I can't. On my body, I feel the gaze of all these different people. I strive to reconnect myself with what I've wanted to say, with sharing the joy of being able to bring these people together to discuss issues I consider relevant. Yet, these previously clearly articulated thoughts and feelings are distant now, they are dwelling somewhere else. I finally start to speak, but I hardly know what I am saying.

The narrator went on to explain that, from her perspective, the room signified disregard on the part of the conference organizers for the innovative work she and her colleague had been doing. The organizers had promised that a room would be set up especially for the workshop, and that she could have as much time as she needed. The half-day session that she had organized with a number of other presenters had shrunk in time, and the workshop space in the university that was hosting the conference had mutated into a high school computer room at the periphery of the conference venue.

How might we think about this computer room and its second or psychic skin? How does that skin work on the narrator to shut down her affect, depriving her of speech and of the ideas she feels passionate about? The second skin exists in this story as writings and images on the walls of the computer room, and in the computers themselves arranged in the rigidly structured space they require. This second skin is not hers, cannot be hers. She experiences the second skin holding within it an active opposition to the innovative workshop she has planned. It holds memories of what is right, approved and accepted. It acts as a hologram of the dominant order, existing on more than the flat surfaces of the walls. The computers are active in creating the psychic skin of this room. They evoke the lives of the high school students who have worked on them—they hold past identities subordinated to school authorities, lacking autonomy and agency. They invoke the narrator's old anxieties of not knowing enough, of being the other to her teachers who possessed knowledge. The space asks of her, in effect, who do you think you are to be generating these new ideas, as if you were a legitimate academic, as if you had authority to speak differently against the grain of dominant discourse?

The posters on the walls, put there by other presenters at the conference, narrate what any legitimate academic would produce. They tell her they cannot tolerate her difference:

> It is as if the forces of knowledge and power cannot tolerate difference—the new, the unthought, the outside—and do all they can to suppress it, by forcing it to conform to expectation, to fit into a structure, to be absorbable, assimilable, and digestible without disturbance or perturbation. (Grosz, 2001: 64)

The history of difficulties in negotiating a time and a space for the workshop permeate the second skin of the room, and confirm for the narrator her own powerlessness, producing her inability to speak something new. In this story the anonymous conference committee and their decisions about her work are like invisible fibers interwoven into the skin of the room. Further, the room is filled up with diverse others, some with an intimate history with the narrator, some known to be "experts." The relational lines are complex and threatening. How can anyone speak to so many different kinds of people at once? How can the new thing-to-be-spoken find a way to emerge into this space?

As Susanne pointed out in her chapter on difference as ethical encounter, with her example of the apology to the stolen generations, pedagogy does not take place only in classrooms. Our next story takes place in the home of a professor where the relations among the participants were not shaped by formal pedagogical codes—not by the materiality of walls, blinds and posters—but by "the quality and intensity of the links established and the experiences activated within that place" which create "links with other fields of knowledge, other ways of thinking, and other identities" (Ceppi and Zini, 1998: n.p.). These students, postgraduates gathered together from all parts of the globe, became one with the house in the shared tasks of preparing food, and of engaging in hospitality. The second skin here, created by the hospitable everyday life of the teacher, and also of the visiting students, their coats and their boots, welcomes the narrator. There is no barrier holding her out, or holding her in. The relationality of the students flourishes in this space, their multiple differences becoming part of the magic of the place and of the event that invites the narrator in, enfolding her in its richness of light, and fabric and human relations:

SECOND SKIN: THE ARCHITECTURE OF PEDAGOGICAL ENCOUNTERS

The tall thin house was easy to find, in a street of other tall thin houses in an old part of the city. The door was open, tulips in tubs on the steps, and she could hear the hum inside from the street. She entered a labyrinth of tiny passages, corners and stairways; brushed past hooks hung with coats and scarves, bundles of shoes on the floor; wandered through rooms of Afghan floor cushions, Turkish rugs, paintings and wall tapestries, with animated women in little clusters everywhere. Dalia from Colombia and Brenda from San Francisco sat shelling peas into a huge earthenware bowl. Fadia from Algeria and Lilian from Cote d'Ivoire, her new housemates in Bremen, were already here. And there was Helen who she'd taught once in a high school in Australia, washing strawberries in a colander at the sink. Bella from Zambia and Barbara, their Dean, leaned against the kitchen cupboards, talking and waving their hands around. Red-headed Cristina from Rio offered her a drink. Knives flashed on chopping boards slicing carrots wielded by women she didn't know and someone whose name she didn't yet remember smiled hello to her and went back to grating cheese. There was Linda their tutor talking with some other women. Fatima from Sweden and Iran, talking with Sadia from Palestine, who later made her cry with a song on a tram late one night, and there was Charlotte from Nigeria wearing one of her gorgeous turbans. And Cally from Perth. Belinda, her German friend, took her down into the back garden where herbs and flowers tangled together in wild profusion and Dania from Tel Aviv waved down through the window, framed by the ivy that crawled up the back wall. There seemed to be room for everybody here.

The participants in this event have created a "Community in the sense of sharing, conviviality, pleasure, well-being, and a sense of belonging for all those involved," it is "a form and quality of space that fosters encounters, exchange, empathy and reciprocity" (Ceppi and Zini, 1998: n.p.).

This transformation of a place into a space where community is able to emerge with all its relational possibilities is an ideal of Reggio Emilia architecture. The place of the teacher's home, in this story, has become a relational space, that is, a space which is stimulating and productive of new relations and affects, a space in which life takes place. As Ceppi and Zini (1998: n.p.) observe: "When we talk about relational space, we mean an integrated space in which the qualities are not strictly aesthetic but are more closely related to 'performance' features." The participants' diversity is enacted in the movable texture of the professor's house creating both open and relational space, where everybody is welcome;

their diversity does not exist in pre-determined, hierarchical and rigid structures but in an active generation of sensory networks—each student is a network spreading out into other networks.

Ceppi's and Zini's emphasis on soft, open, movable space resonates with Deleuze's and Guattari's (1987) distinction between smooth and striated space. As we have explored in previous chapters, smooth space is the "space of intensive processes and assemblages, as opposed to the striated space of stratified or stable systems" (Bonta and Protevi, 2004: 114). Striations are associated with stratification, centralization, hierarchization, and the freezing of the flow of elements, bodies, and emotions. The professor's house enables bodies, experiences, tastes, senses and desires, to move freely in various directions; there are no hierarchies, no centers in the house; it does not determine the connections and meeting points but makes them possible.

The excess and permeability of this evening event, fold back into the daytime spaces of learning and teaching. The narrator eases herself into this serene and amiable scene where boundaries dissolve, where habitual repetitions can be interrupted, where borders between old territories shift and dissolve, where lines of flight become possible.

In the next story the narrator tells of an intense teaching experience. She was with the students for a two-day course, and she found them to be dynamic, cooperative and quick-witted in the pedagogical space they created together. She writes about one particular moment, where her own boundaries were undone and she became one with her written materials up on the wall. It is an ecstatic moment in which she stands outside herself, outside the molar striations of normal and normative everyday pedagogy:

I am reading aloud the enigmatic verses on the projector screen to the students to show them how to do the interpretive work. The students are sitting in a long rectangle in front of the place where I am standing, but I have my back turned to them at that particular moment. I am beginning with my interpretation and it goes so easily, the stream of words is emerging from my mouth, they are sliding out effortlessly. I am listening to my voice pronouncing the words and I am aware of its surprising continuity. Suddenly, I am losing contact with myself as a speaker and I am drawn into the lines on the projector screen. I am becoming the words I am articulating, I am between and inside of them. The words on the screen interweave with my voice and together, they attract me, fascinate me, they hold me in their reach. It is an ecstatic moment, a strong pleasure in letting oneself go. I can hear that my voice is trembling. It is only a short moment and then I am back in the classroom again and I know that I need to turn back and to face my students who have witnessed it all. I feel close to them, and yet, I am also embarrassed for being so unexpectedly out of control.

This is a moving moment for the teacher, who draws the students with her in that movement—in that moment of dissolving boundaries and openness to the not-yet-known. The words on the wall flow off the wall and enter them, enfolding all of them in their sensual and pleasurable embrace. Teacher and students are not separated but have become, in those two days, no longer strangers. They are caught up in the mutual exploration of ideas where thinking and being cannot be separated (Nancy, 2000). The narrator feels the projector screen and the words written on it as her own second skin. She produces them and endows them with life by reading them aloud to the students. As her reading proceeds, the separation between herself and the second skin made up of the writing on the wall vanishes. Their merging brings ecstasy and pleasure. But she feels there is something shameful in such an ecstatic mo(ve)ment. The loss of borders between herself and the outside object (the screen, the writing), the de-territorialization of the striated spaces potentially robs her of the agency that is lodged in those striations. She is afraid that the emotion she feels entails a loss of her capacity to be a complete and rational subject. The association of science and scientists with the wholly rational, with the not-emotional, can only be momentarily undone. While neuroscientists have demonstrated that rationality is absolutely dependent on emotion (Lehrer, 2007), the habituated repetitions and the categories that we have historically come to know ourselves through, as Susanne shows in her chapter, are not easily undone. Nevertheless, in that moment of being undone, the narrator enters the smooth space that is also a space of relationality, a space of being *with-writing, with-others*; of *becoming-other*:

> Becoming is what enables a trait, a line, an orientation, an event to be released from the system, series, organism, or object that may have the effect of transformation of the whole, making it no longer function singularly: it is an encounter between bodies that releases something from each and, in the process, releases or makes real a virtuality, a series of enabling and transforming possibilities. (Grosz, 2001: 70)

The next story is also one of pedagogical bliss. The narrator is again in a conference room in front of a largely unknown audience. She feels the room change shape as she moves, like Oddbod and Blossom in an earlier chapter, from her initial anxiety into an intimate and satisfying encounter with her listeners.

I am the second-last speaker and it's been a long day. I have been through all the nerves and the nervousness. Now it's just the time to do it. As I begin, I know that it is more than good enough, very relevant, on matters yet untouched. I am not self-congratulatory, just confident. A much happier way to be than my usual doubts. But then I am reading the part which I wrote as a story. And the atmosphere tips. It tips and slides into something completely unknown. I look up briefly to know what is different in the room and I ask myself, 'did I imagine people were sitting on the edges of their chairs? Is the room physically smaller now, more intimate? Can it be true that they are as if gripped by these words?' I continue reading the story, but cautiously, each word dropping gently into open hearts. I am in a new place, a new space, feeling my way.

The story pulls the audience into the ambience of its words. The shift created in the room through that engagement propels her into a new space, one which she does not recall experiencing before in the striated spaces of the academy. But now she is conscious of a different kind of reception, a different kind of speaking. As in the previous story, there is a relationality between the words, her being and the being of her listeners. It is an experience of connectedness and mutual affect, linking speaker, audience and words in a becoming-story in which "the identity of the self is lost...to the advantage of an intense multiplicity and a power of metamorphosis" (Deleuze, 1990: 297). The narrator's strategy of attention that is mirrored by her listeners, echoes the strategy of attention that Constance elaborated in her chapter on listening. It makes possible a mutual act of listening that, in Rinaldi's words, "creates a deep opening":

> [L]istening is an attitude that requires the courage to abandon yourself to the conviction that our being is just a small part of a broader knowledge; listening is a metaphor for openness to others, sensitivity to listen and be listened to, with all your senses...Behind each act of listening there is desire, emotion, openness to differences, to different values and points of view... Competent listening creates a deep opening and predisposition toward change. (Rinaldi, 2006: 114)

SECOND SKIN: THE ARCHITECTURE OF PEDAGOGICAL ENCOUNTERS

In such ecstatic moments when old boundaries are dissolved and when new ideas are opened up, the speaker and listener affirm each other. The space they create between them and among them is smooth in the Deleuzian sense—it is mobile, not caught in rigid striations, not caught in categorical difference, but open to differenciation, to "continuous difference/multiplicity...to intensities, and to evolution rather than succession" (Massey, 2005: 21). Teachers and students together are caught up together in a line of flight, and a moment of affirmation.

Our final story in this chapter—and in this book—moves to the idea, so strongly expressed in Reggio Emilia writing, that the boundaries between inside and outside should be dissolved: "a school should not be a sort of counter-world, but the essence and distillation of society. Contemporary reality can and should permeate the school, filtered by a cultural project of interpretation that serves as membrane and interface" (Ceppi and Zini, 1998: n.p.). This story reflects the complex pedagogical work of linking teaching-learning spaces with the community outside the tertiary classroom and the multi-logic nature of such a space. In this story the teacher enters the room first to find it haunted by the traces of her previous classes: art works, performances and 3D installations. The story ends with a coda where the students work collaboratively to reanimate the second skin that lingers in that space, within which they are brought together. The memories of what they came to understand through this work are evoked as a living present skin. The holographic qualities of memory mean that the room itself, even without the art works, still holds the works and the new knowledges they carried.

I open the classroom door. The room is bare, empty of students. It is a drama room. Black walls and curtains and scratched varnished floorboards. White lockers line one wall only half way up, windows above them reveal barely visible tree tops. Whiteboards line another wall, a few long tables in front of them. Stacks of chairs crowd into the corners. I walk inside, my folder brimming with semester-long teaching content: 12 weeks of making art together in community, 12 weeks of critical reflection and theorizing about art in individual and social change. I stand in the silence and listen. I hear voices hum, see vibrant colors splashed in paintings and posters against the walls. An installation of black curtains hangs from the ceiling, someone sits inside surrounded by the despair of depression, an extra large cardboard box is on its side open ended against the wall with lonely belongings tidied inside and a small handwritten note on the outside, 'this is my home, I am someone's daughter, someone's son'. I hear music, clear melodies rise into the space singing the heartache of the abused child. A screen tells a story in images of the changing nature of a local community from bushland to corporate business centre, and on a table beside it, a 3D collage asks questions about the corporatization of child care. My skin tingles and my heart is paradoxically empty/full. I am hearing the absent presence of the previous week's assessment task in which three successive groups of 30 students have filled the room with their imaginative representations of social issues about which they are passionate and in which they would like to see social and political change.

The students arrive for class and we sit together in a circle and reflect on the previous week's marketplace of social issues and imagination in action. Slowly the dynamic resonance of our shared passion for social and political change reverberates into the classroom so that even the bare walls sing.

This university classroom as a physical space is reminiscent of the art classroom in which we held our art workshop, and of the hall in which Oddbod's and Blossom's drama workshops took place. Its old worn surfaces are open to the inscriptions of the passions and commitments of teacher and both past and present students. There is a bareness but also an invitation to use the space in creative ways. It does not reject the possibility of opening up thought within it, drawing on the threads of connection with each autobiographical trajectory and with the intermeshing of lives outside itself. Its second skin is in-formed by the relationality of art making in community which Catherine explored in her chapter on relationality and the art of becoming. The teacher actively envisages the space itself as having a history and a relationship with her. It becomes a "place for the alchemic composition of knowledge and desires, for perceiving and constructing reality" (Ceppi and Zini, 1998: n.p.). Central to this teacher's work is the emphasis on diversity and movement that were elaborated in Bronwyn's chapter on difference and differenciation, and on the other's difference as a value. The other, in her difference, is a valuable extension of singular/plural space of the classroom—to be welcomed—an enrichment of the networks of meaning through which each singular/plural self comes to exist.

> Controversy and the conflict of ideas play a fundamental role in this system, bringing out the significant aspects of individual thought and at the same time giving new meaning to the knowledge-building process. This is because

knowledge develops much more within a context of diversity rather than one of homogeneity, and also because in situations of conflicting interpretations, the need to argue your own point of view is the catalyst for the fundamental process of metacognition (knowledge of knowledge), providing an opportunity for 're-knowing' your knowledge in a different light, enriched by the new and different opinions offered by others. (Rinaldi, 2006: 127)

(In)conclusion

Throughout this book we have explored pedagogical encounters using our own memory stories and ethnographic stories to bring elements of Deleuzian thought into our thinking about pedagogy and place. Provocations and inspirations from Reggio Emilia educational philosophy and practice have provided the other significant source of our investigations into the interrelations between place and pedagogical encounters. We have unfolded here the possibilities of learning, in a Deleuzian sense, as an aspiration towards new thought that is more like an opening towards an unpredictable line of flight than an auditable product or outcome. We have fleshed out with our stories a model of learning as transformative, not just for students but also for teachers. The teaching-learning spaces that we have re-membered are oriented towards the art of becoming, where becoming is a continuous process of differenciation beginning as: "a moment of de-individualization" and accompanied by "new ways of being in the world, new ways of thinking and feeling" (Roffe, 2007: 43) for teachers and students.

As most of the stories we have examined in this book demonstrate, smooth spaces are always already implicated in striated spaces. The pedagogical sites we have visited include the striations of a Year Ten distance education syllabus, an early literacy outcome that had to be ticked off, a marking rubric and assessment task, a public performance as a result of a drama course, the completion of an art work, and finally, university tutorials and conference presentations. It is with/in the striations of consistent routine, materials, pedagogies and people, that smooth spaces appear, where Jaydana can begin to acquire a sense of herself as someone worth listening to, or where Kiet can work her way through paint and paper to a sense of competence and inclusion, where students from other lands and with other languages can find a means to move their peers and their teacher toward new ways of understanding difference, and where the clowns can emerge beyond their terror. In their moments of flight they each hold onto a "small plot of land" (Deleuze and

Guattari, 1987: 161), a safe and predictable space, a space that opens up the possibility of differenciation, of "continuous difference/multiplicity... [of] inten-sities, and [of] evolution rather than succession" (Massey, 2005: 21).

Not all striations are benign. The technologies of neoliberalism, as discussed at the beginning of this book, can be suffocating; they can close things down. Where this is so, we must work to keep pedagogical spaces open to the future "however much we [or others] might try to close them" (Massey, 2005: 180).

Classrooms are marked by "throwntogetherness," to borrow Massey's term, and it is in this necessary idiosyncrasy and unpredictability that the "challenge of negotiating a here-and-now...within and between both human and non-human" arises (Massey, 2005: 140). Pedagogical encounters arise in relations between human and nonhuman, animate and inanimate, one and the other, where agency lies not in controlling each of the others but in openness to the other and to the not-yet-known. The boundaries between objects and the self are looser than they have been made to appear in past constructions of human subjects and of pedagogy. As children play with materials that are at hand, gender performances shift, things mutate, a boy's arm and a bag of potatoes merge to become a centrifuge, they learn something new about relational and material beings. In the art of becoming, materials themselves are active agents in the process; in our art workshop the fall and tear of silk— or the intransigence of tin—dictated the next move to the art maker, mobilizing an aesthetic sense that is more affect than reason.

The pedagogical encounters that we explore in this book link artistic becoming with transformative learning for both students and teachers. Openings arose in free play with costumes for the clowns Blossom and Oddbod, and for George in his yellow butterfly skirt; they arose in play with sand and water and paint and other materials; in performance and in poetry; they arose in listening to and valuing the difference of the other. In each of these examples the final works—the "art object" or "the work"—mattered less than the process, the moments of becoming, the shifts that were enabled with/in the community of teacher-learners.

Art in a Deleuzian paradigm is "the art of affect more than representation, a system of dynamized and impacting forces rather than a system of unique images that function under the regime of signs" (Grosz, 2008a: 3). As such art—its making and its reception—is located and experienced in the body, where affect registers. Art, in Grosz's definition includes "all forms of creativity or production that generate intensity, sensation, or affect: music, painting, sculpture, literature, architecture, design, landscape, dance, performance, and so on" (Grosz, 2008a: 3). In the pedagogical encounters in this book where students experimented with art and with art materials, or where they chose their own form or mode of response as they do in the final story in this chapter, affective responses are anticipated and welcomed. These encounters are marked not by difference as discrete categorical difference but by difference as a continuing process of differenciation, of becoming, where each subject is a sensory and meaning network, radiating out into other networks.

Affect is a critical notion for understanding pedagogy and its effects and potentials as we have explored them through this book. Pedagogical encounters as we are theorizing them in this book involve learning as a transformative practice for teachers and students. They move us (physically and emotionally) from one place to another. The notion of affect brings together physical, emotional and sensory dimensions of embodiment with movement. The teacher's work is not to contain, or shape, or control, or to organize the students to produce predetermined outcomes, but to invoke a particular "capacity: affect as a *response to*" (Biddle, 2007: 15). Biddle describes this as:

> ...a reaction, involuntary, often unconscious, that is at once physiological, material and social; a quickening of the heart, an intake of the breath, a tensing of muscles, interest itself: affect is the register of our embodied encounter with the world. Affect tells us that we are sensory beings who feel, sense, smell—respond—as a primary mode of engagement. (Biddle, 2007: 15)

Affect operates in excess of consciousness: it seems individual but is also profoundly social, able to be conveyed through the body to others, even contagious. It accounts for repulsion as well as attraction and, as it focuses on the concrete and the lived and our "responses to," can help explain the dulling effect of one architectural space and the transcendence of another, or how an unpromising space is transformed by the relations within it. Biddle calls affect "switch-like" (2007: 17), and as such it can account for the rapid shift that happens in several stories in this chapter when people move from one physical space into another. For transformative learning, attention must be paid to the aesthetic, affective and relational dimensions of pedagogical encounters.

The work of the teacher is not that of benign or passive facilitation, allowing learners to find their own way, but an artful and deeply responsive and engaged practice. The stories that we have explored in this book provide many instances of teachers who know what to do, or what particular thing to provide at the point of need for each of the learners in their charge. Our art workshop provided the most detailed glimpses into this pedagogical art, where our teachers, who were not yet officially qualified, moved continuously and discreetly amongst their struggling art students, providing a suggestion to one person, a button to another, a new technique to another. Jade and Alicia took up what we call a strategy of attention. This strategy of attention is responsive to and gives rise to differenciation, to the becomings of each of the learners in the pedagogical space in their own particular and supported way. The teacher in the classroom of Aboriginal children that Susanne narrates has students working on all sorts of language rich projects around the room as she moves from one to the other, informally monitoring their progress and trying to provide what each student needs. Catherine's and Constance's drama teacher, Bridget, points her student towards the costume room and invites her to find her song, maintaining an insistence that she will find the capacity to participate. She brings the rest of the class into the community in which the pedagogical encounter is made possible. Teacher and students together take up a strategy of attention that enables Blossom to move beyond her fears.

The final element of pedagogical encounters that we wish to highlight in this book is the ethics of encounter. Ethical relationality lies at the heart of those pedagogical encounters that enable the art of becoming. As we discussed at the beginning of this book, neoliberal impacts on education have brought with them an obsession with auditable outcomes and testing regimes that may run counter to an ethical relationality. In Constance's story of homeless youth, an ethical relationality is in the quality of engagement that the teacher, Jo, provides, the unconditional and personable interest and concern that she shows for each student that they most appreciate. Her regard for them (as well as the clarity of her rules) is unwavering and, because of this, it is reciprocated by the students, even though it is not easy for them, given their addictions and the complications of their lives. Susanne documents moments of affective and embodied connection across racial and linguistic difference that destabilize authority and move the teacher, with her students, to new understandings of themselves and others in the world. In both of these chapters, the classroom is part of and permeated by the world, while it also aims to provide a safer space away from the world. An ethics of pedagogical encounter takes into account the inequities of socio-historical contexts and entails an embodied vulnerability and responsibility to and for the other that rewrites the role of the teacher. Listening is again at the centre of such an ethical encounter, and community, albeit contingent and transient, is its goal. Listening, for each teacher, is an act of becoming where the teacher lets go of some aspect of her own individuality and at the same time opens up for herself new ways of seeing and being.

While we have been writing this book, and prior to that in our research grouping, we have also aimed for community. Although our group has scattered since we began this project, with Katerina returned to the Czech Republic and Constance relocated to Melbourne, we have endeavored to continue listening and reading and attending to one another. We have formed and reformed ourselves into community in specific temporal and geophysical spaces—a house by the sea, an art room, hunched over our separate computers; we have worked to create and maintain relations among us that reflect the pedagogical encounters that we believe have had the most profound effects on ourselves as learners, as teachers, as researchers. We hope that the stories and analyses in this book have resonated with you, our readers—and that we have brought you, in the spaces of your reading, into our community of thought and practice.

Bibliography

ABC online forum. (2008) Transcript of ABC Panel Discussion on Youth Homelessness. Online. Available HTTP: <http://www.abc.net.au/tv/oasis/report/report.htm> (accessed 7 March 2009).
ABC Television. (2008) The Oasis-synopsis. Online. Available HTTP: <http://www.abc.net.au/tv/oasis/about/synopsis.htm> (accessed 7 March 2009).
Ahmed, S. (2000) *Strange encounters: Embodied others in post-coloniality*, London: Routledge.
Alaimo, S. and Hekman, S. (2008) 'Introduction: Emerging models of materiality in feminist theory', in S. Alaimo and S. Hekman (eds.) *Material feminisms*, Bloomington: Indiana University Press. 1–22.
Albrecht-Crane, C. and Slack, J. D. (2003) 'Toward a pedagogy of affect', in J. D. Slack (ed.) *Animations of Deleuze and Guattari*, New York: Peter Lang Publishing. 191–216.
—— (2007) 'Toward a pedagogy of affect', in A. Hickey-Moody and P. Malins (eds.) *Deleuzian encounters. Studies in contemporary social issues*, Houndmills: Palgrave Macmillan. 99–110.
Bell, V. (1996) 'Show and tell: Passing and narrative in Toni Morrison's Jazz', *Social identities*, 2(2). 221–236.
—— (2006) 'Performative knowledge', *Theory, culture and society*, 23 (2–3), 214–217.
—— (2007) *Culture and performance: The challenge of ethics, politics and feminist theory*, Oxford: Berg.
Biddle, J. (2007) *Breasts, bodies, canvas: Central desert art as experience*, Sydney: University of New South Wales Press.
Bion, W. (1961) *Experiences in groups and other papers*, London: Tavistock.
Bonta, M. and Protevi J. (2004) *Deleuze and Geophilosophy: A Guide and Glossary*, Edinburgh: Edinburgh University Press.
Braidotti, R. (2006) *Transpositions*, Cambridge, UK: Polity Press.
Brandon, B. and Batten, F. (1984) 'Drama Action Centre'. Unpublished course brochure.
Buchanan, I and Lambert, G. (2005) 'Introduction', in I. Buchanan and G. Lambert (eds.) *Deleuze and space*, Edinburgh: Edinburgh University Press. 1–15.
Butler, J. (1997) *The Psychic Life of Power: Theories in Subjection*, Stanford, CA: Stanford University Press.
—— (2004) *Precarious life: the powers of mourning and violence*, London & New York: Verso.
—— (2005) *Giving an Account of Oneself*, New York: Fordham University Press Cambridge, MA: MIT press.
Camden Pratt, C. E. (2002) *Daughters of Persephone: legacies of maternal 'madness'*, Unpublished doctoral thesis, University of Western Sydney.

—— (2003) 'Waiting to be re-membered', Art Exhibition, Sydney: Blue Mountains Women's Health Centre.

—— (2006) *Out of the shadows: daughters growing up with a 'mad' mother*, Sydney: Finch Publications.

—— (2007) 'Creative arts and critical autobiography: Challenges of blending the deeply personal and the academic in qualitative research', in J. Higgs, A. Titchen, D. Horsfall and H. B. Armstrong (eds.) *Being Critical and Creative in Qualitative Research*, Sydney: Hampden Press. 248–259.

—— (2008) 'Social Ecology and Creative Pedagogy: using creative arts and critical thinking in co-creating and sustaining ecological learning webs in university pedagogies,' *Transnational Curriculum Inquiry*, 5 (1). Online. Available HTTP: <http://nitinat.library.ubc.ca/ojs/index.php/tci> (accessed 26 January 2009).

Ceppi, G. and Zini, M. (eds.) (1998) *Children, Spaces, Relations. Metaproject for an environment for young children*, Milan: Domus Academy Research Center.

Conley, V. A. (2006) 'Borderlines', in I. Buchanan and A. Parr (eds.) *Deleuze and the contemporary world*, Edinburgh: Edinburgh University Press. 95–107.

Dahlberg, G. and Moss, P. (2005) *Ethics and politics in early childhood education*, London & New York: Routledge/Falmer.

—— (2006) 'Introduction: our Reggio Emilia', in C. Rinaldi *In Dialogue with Reggio Emilia. Listening Researching and Learning*, London: Routledge. 1–22.

Dahlberg, G., Moss, P. and Pence, A. (1999) *Beyond Quality in Early childhood Education and Care*, London: Routledge/Falmer.

Davies, B. (1989) *Frogs and Snails and Feminist Tales. Preschool Children and Gender*, Sydney: Allen and Unwin. 2nd Edition (2003) NJ Cresskill: Hampton Press.

—— (2006). 'Identity, Abjection and Otherness: Creating the self, creating difference', in M. Arnot and M. Mac an Ghaill (eds.) *The Routledge Falmer Reader in Gender and Education*, London: Routledge. 72–90.

—— (2008) 'Re-thinking 'behavior' in terms of positioning and the ethics of responsibility', in A. M. Phelan and J. Sumsion (eds.) *Provoking Absences: Critical Readings in Teacher Education*, Rotterdam: Sense Publishers.

Davies, B. and Bansel, P. (2007a) 'Governmentality and academic work: Shaping the hearts and minds of academic workers', *Journal of Curriculum Theorizing*, 23 (2). 9–26.

—— (2007b) 'Neoliberalism and education', *International Journal of Qualitative Studies in Education*, Special issue on neoliberalism and education, B. Davies and P. Bansel (eds.), 20(3). 247–260.

Davies, B., Browne, J., Gannon, S., Hopkins, L., McCann, H. and Wihlborg, M. (2006) 'Constituting 'the subject' in poststructuralist discourse', *Feminism and Psychology*, 16(1). 87–103. Reprinted in Davies, B. and Gannon, S. (2006) *Doing Collective Biography*. Maidenhead: Open University Press. 167–181.

Davies, B. and Gannon, S. (2006) *Doing Collective Biography*, Maidenhead: Open University Press.

Davies, B., Gottsche, M. and Bansel, P. (2006) 'The rise and fall of the neoliberal university', *European Journal of Education*, 41(2). 305–319.
Davies, B. and Hunt, R. (1994) 'Classroom competencies and marginal positionings', *British Journal of Sociology of Education*, 15(2). 389–408.
Davies, B. and Kasama, H. (2004) *Gender in Japanese Preschools. Frogs and Snails and Feminist Tales in Japan*, NJ: Cresskill, Hampton Press.
Dawe, B. (2006) *Sometimes gladness. Collected poems 1954–2005*, Sydney: Pearson Education.
Deleuze, G. (1983) *Nietzsche and philosophy*, London: Athlone Press.
—— (1988) *Bergsonism*, New York: Zone Books.
—— (1990) *The Logic of Sense*, trans M. Lester & C. Stivale. New York: Columbia University Press.
—— (1994) *Difference and repetition*, New York: Columbia University Press.
—— (1995) *Negotiations 1972-1990*, New York: Columbia University Press.
Deleuze, G. and Guattari, F. (1987) *A Thousand Plateaus: Capitalism and Schizophrenia*, London: Athlone Press.
Deleuze, G. and Parnet, C. (1987) *Dialogues*, New York: Columbia University Press.
—— (2002) *Dialogues II*, New York: Columbia University Press.
Diprose, R. (2001) 'Bearing witness to cultural difference, with apology to Levinas', *Angelaki: Journal of the theoretical humanities*, 6(2). 125–135.
Dusseldorp Skills Forum (DSF) (2007) *How young people are faring 2007: At a glance*, Sydney: Dusseldorp Skills Forum.
Ellsworth, E. (2005) *Places of Learning. Media, Architecture, Learning*, New York: Routledge/Falmer.
Ellwood, C. (2006) 'Homelessness, drugs, wounds, and transformations', paper given at the *Reclaiming the Margins: Youth, research, activism* conference, Sydney, 3–4 November.
Foucault, M. (1977) 'Theatrum philosophicaum', in D. Bouchard (ed.) *Language, counter-memory, practice: selected essays and interviews*, Ithaca, N.Y.: Cornell University Press.
—— (1992) *The History of Sexuality: the use of pleasure (Vol. 2)*, London: Penguin.
—— (2003) *Society must be defended*, Lectures at the College de France 1975–76, New York: Picador.
Fox, J. (ed.). (1987) *The Essential Moreno*, New York: Springer Publishing Company.
Gannon, S. (2008) 'Inhabiting silence: A sorry story', *LEARNing landscapes: Education and the arts*, 3. Online. Available HTTP: <http://www.learnquebec.ca/en/content/learninglandscapes/index.html> (accessed 10 February 2009).
Grosz, E. (1994) 'A thousand tiny sexes: feminism and rhizomatics', in C. V. Boundas and D. Olkowski (eds.) *Gilles Deleuze and the theatre of philosophy*, New York: Routledge.
—— (2001) *Architecture from the Outside. Essays in Virtual and Real Space*, Massachusetts: The MIT Press.

—— (2008a) *Chaos, Territory, Art. Deleuze and the Framing of the Earth*, New York: Columbia University Press.
—— (2008b) 'Darwin and feminism: Preliminary investigations for a possible alliance', in S. Alaimo and S. Hekman (eds.) *Material feminisms*, Bloomington: Indiana University Press. 23–51.
Guattari, F. and Bains, P. (1995) *Chaosmosis: an ethico-aesthetic paradigm*, Bloomington: Indiana University Press.
Hallward, P. (2003) "Everything is real': Gilles Deleuze and creative univocity', *New Formations*, 49 (Spring). 61–74.
Halsey, M. (2007) 'Molar ecology: what can the (full) body of an eco-tourist do?', in A. Hickey-Moody and P. Malins (eds.) *Deleuzian Encounters. Studies in Contemporary Social Issues*, Houndmills: Palgrave Macmillan. 135–150.
Herrera, H. (1983) *Frida: A biography of Frida Kahlo*. New York: Harper and Rowe.
Hickey-Moody, A. and Malins, P. (2007). 'Introduction: Gilles Deleuze and four movements in social thought', in A. Hickey-Moody and P. Malins (eds.) *Deleuzian encounters. Studies in contemporary social issues*, Houndmills: Palgrave Macmillan. 1–24.
Holmes, P. (1991) 'Classical psychodrama: An overview', in P. Holmes and M. Karp (eds.) *Psychodrama: Inspiration and technique*, London & New York: Tavistock/Routledge. 7–13.
hooks, b. (1994) *Teaching to transgress*, New York: Routledge.
Horsfall, D., Bridgeman, K., Camden-Pratt, C., Kaufman Hall, V. and Pinn, J. (2007) 'Playing Creative Edges : Performing Research - Women out to Lunch', in J. Higgs, A. Tichen, D. Horsfall and H. B. Armstrong (eds.) *Being Critical and Creative in Qualitative Research*, Sydney: Hampden Press. 136–151.
Latour, B. (2005) *Reassembling the social. An Introduction to Actor-Network-Theory*, Oxford: Oxford University Press.
Lampert, J. (2009) *Children's fiction about 9/11*, New York: Routledge.
LeCoq, J., Carasso, J.G. and Lallias, J.C. (2001) *The Moving Body*, New York: Routledge.
Lehrer, J. (2007) *Proust was a Neuroscientist*, Boston: Houghton Mifflin Company.
Lenz Taguchi, H. (2009/ forthcoming) *Going beyond the theory/practice divide in early childhood education: Introducing an intra-active pedagogy*, Routledge/Falmer Press.
Lyotard, J-F. (1979/84) *The Postmodern Condition: A Report on Knowledge*, Manchester: Manchester University Press.
Macy, J. (1991) *World as lover, world as self*, Berkeley: Parallax.
Malins, P. (2007) 'City folds: injecting drug use and urban space', in A. Hickey-Moody and P. Malins (eds.) *Deleuzian Encounters. Studies in Contemporary Social Issues*, Houndmills: Palgrave Macmillan. 151–168.
Massey, D. (2005) *For space*, London: Sage.
May, T. (1997) *Reconsidering difference: Nancy, Derrida, Levinas and Deleuze*, Philadelphia: Pennsylvania State University Press.
Merleau-Ponty, M. (1964) *Signs*, Evanston, IL: Northwestern University Press.

BIBLIOGRAPHY

Moreno, J. (1953) *Who Shall Survive?* New York: Beacon House.
Moss, P. and Petrie, P. (2002) *From Children's Services to Children's Spaces: Public Policy, Children and Childhood*, London: Routledge/Falmer.
Nancy, J. L. (2000) *Of being singular plural*, Stanford, CA: Stanford University Press.
NSW Department of Education and Training. (2008) NSW Public Schools: The School Certificate. Online. Available: HTTP: <http://www.schools.nsw.edu.au/learning/7-12assessments/schoolcertificate.php> (accessed 7 March 2009).
O'Connor, B. (2001). 'Mapping training/mapping performance: Current trends in Australian actor training', in I. Watson (ed.) *Performer training: Developments across cultures*, London: Routledge. 47–60.
Patton, P. (2007) 'Preface', in A. Hickey-Moody and P. Malins (eds.) *Deleuzian Encounters. Studies in Contemporary Social Issues*, Houndmills: Palgrave Macmillan. ix–x.
Phelan, A. M. and Sumsion, J. (eds.) (2008) *Provoking Absences: Critical Readings in Teacher Education*, Rotterdam: Sense Publishers.
Reynolds, W. and Webber, J. (2004) 'Introduction', in W. Reynolds and J. Webber (eds.) *Expanding curriculum theory: Dis/positions and lines of flight*, Mahwah, NJ: Lawrence Erlbaum Associates. 1–18.
Rinaldi, C. (2006) *In Dialogue with Reggio Emilia. Listening, Researching and Learning*, London: Routledge.
Roffe, J. (2007) 'Politics beyond identity', in A. Hickey-Moody and P. Malins (eds.) *Deleuzian encounters. Studies in contemporary social issues*, Houndmills: Palgrave Macmillan. 40–49.
Roy, K. (2004) 'Overcoming Nihilism: From communication to Deleuzian expression', *Educational philosophy and theory*, 36 (3). 297–312.
—— (2005) 'Power and resistance: insurgent spaces, Deleuze, and curriculum', *Journal of Curriculum Theorizing*, 21 (1). 27–38.
Rudd, K. (2008) Speech. 'Apology to Australia's indigenous peoples'. Online. Available HTTP: <http://www.pm.gov.au/media/Speech/2008/speech_0073.cfm> (accessed 7 March 2009).
—— (2009) 'The global financial crisis', *The Monthly: Australian Politics, Society and Culture*, February, 42.
Schacht, M. (2007) 'Spontaneity-creativity: The psychodramatic concept of change', in C. Baim, J. Burmeister and M. Maciel (eds.) *Psychodrama: Advances in theory and practice*, London & New York: Routledge. 21–39.
Somerville, M. (2008) 'A Place Pedagogy for 'Global Contemporaneity'', *Educational Philosophy and Theory*, 40. 1–19.
Springgay, S. (2008) *Body knowledge and curriculum. Pedagogies of touch in youth and visual culture*, New York: Peter Lang.
Stivale, C. (1998) *The two-fold thought of Deleuze and Guattari*, New York: Guilford Press.
Sweet, R. (2006) 'Education, training and employment in an international perspective', Paper presented at *New transitions: Challenges facing Australian youth* conference, Melbourne, 18 August.

Todd, S. (2003) *Learning from the other. Levinas, psychoanalysis, and ethical possibilities in education*, New York: State University of New York Press.

Weiss, G. (1999) *Body image: Embodiment as intercoporeality*, New York: Routledge.

Williams, J. (2003) *Gilles Deleuze's 'Difference and repetition': a critical introduction and guide*, Edinburgh: Edinburgh University Press.

Wilson, E. A. (2004). *Psychosomatic. Feminism and the Neurological Body*, Durham: Duke University Press.

Woodward, A. (2007) 'Deleuze and suicide', in A. Hickey-Moody and P. Malins (eds.) *Deleuzian Encounters. Studies in Contemporary Social Issues*, Houndmills: Palgrave Macmillan. 62–75.

Wright, J. (2001) 'The masks of Jaques LeCoq', in F. Chamberlain and R. Yarrow (eds.) *Jaques LeCoq and the British Theatre*, London and New York: Routledge. 71–84.

Youdell, D. (2006) *Impossible bodies, impossible selves: Exclusion and student subjectivities*, Dordrecht: Springer.

Yunupingu, G. (2008) 'Tradition, truth and tomorrow: A memoir', *The Monthly: Australian Politics, Society and Culture*, December 2008–January 2009, 41.

Katerina, Constance, Bronwyn, Catherine & Susanne at Bombo Beach

LIST OF AUTHORS

PROFESSOR BRONWYN DAVIES *(editor/author)* is an independent scholar based in Sydney, Australia. She is also a Professorial Fellow at the University of Melbourne. The distinctive features of her work are, on the one hand, her development of innovative social science research methodologies incorporating elements of the visual, literary and performative arts, and, on the other, its strong base in the conceptual work of poststructuralist philosophers such as Deleuze, Foucault and Nancy. Her research explores the discursive practices and relations of power through which particular social worlds are constituted. She is well known for her work on gender, for her work with collective biography, and for her writing on poststructuralist theory.

DR SUSANNE GANNON *(editor/author)* is a Senior Lecturer in English education at the University of Western Sydney. She has published in diverse areas including feminist and poststructural research methodologies, English and literacy education, creative writing and poetic representation. She is the author of *Flesh and the text: Poststructural theory and writing research* (2008) and co-editor with Professor Davies of *Doing collective biography* (2006). She was a high school teacher and curriculum adviser for more than fifteen years before beginning a university career. She maintains close relationships with secondary schools through her teaching and research.

DR PETER BANSEL *(author)* is currently a Research Fellow with the Centre for Educational Research at the University of Western Sydney. He has taught in early childhood and primary school settings and has lectured for more than ten years at a number of universities in areas including education, literature and critical psychology. His interest in the application of poststructural philosophical theory to empirical research is evident across his publications.

DR CATHERINE CAMDEN PRATT *(author)* lectures in social ecology and in education at the University of Western Sydney. She also worked as a primary school teacher and consultant in a variety of educational settings for twenty years. She is a recipient of a teaching award for outstanding pedagogy at University level. Her interests in arts-based research methodologies and critical autobiography are evidenced in her teaching and in a number of research publications, including her book *Daughters of Persephone: Daughters growing up with a 'mad' mother* (2006).

DR CONSTANCE ELLWOOD *(author)* currently lectures in communication skills to undergraduate medical and dentistry students at the University of Melbourne. She has been a TESOL and literacy teacher in a range of educational sectors for over twenty years and was a joint recipient of a team award for excellence in teaching at tertiary level. She has worked with Deleuzian poststructural philosophy and questions of 'difference' for many years.

DR KATERINA ZABRODSKA *(author)* has recently completed a PhD in social psychology at Masaryk University, Czech Republic. She has achieved a number of awards through her studies, including an Endeavour Europe Award to work at the University of Western Sydney. She has just published the first original book on poststructural discourse analysis and gender in the Czech language, *Variace na gender: Poststrukturalismus, diskurzivní analýza a genderová identita / Variations on the theme of gender: Poststructuralism, discourse analysis and gender identity* (2009). She has taught discourse analysis and qualitative methodology at tertiary level for several years in the Czech Republic.

INDEX

A

Aboriginal
  students 68–71, 79–83
  politics 83, 85, 87
  teaching 115–118, 148

Ahmed 14, 102
  embodied encounter 70–71, 74, 76–77, 81
  ethical encounter 78, 84, 91
  difference 87

apology 71, 84–87, 138

architecture, architectural 6–7, 26, 131–134, 147

art 1–2, 11–12, 14–16, 26, 69–88, 134, 143–148
  art making 14–15, 144, 146
    child 53–56, 60–67
    adult 105–130

assemblage 9, 12, 16, 86, 120, 140
  Deleuzian 24, 71, 73, 88

attention
  strategies of 13, 15, 33–34, 42–47, 50–51, 55, 64–65, 93, 129, 142, 148
  close 9, 94

B

becoming
  art of 17, 34, 66, 68, 70, 145–146
  becoming-other 23, 76, 141
  fluid becoming 19, 102, 125

being-with 64, 99, 102, 141

Bell 14, 69, 71–74, 82–83, 85, 88

Braidotti 28–29, 73, 100

Butler 10, 34, 37, 100

C

capitalism 2–5, 16

Ceppi and Zini 8, 33–35, 60, 65–66, 89–93, 131, 138–140
  Reggio Emilia 6–7, 11–12, 35, 43–44, 133, 135, 143–144
  second skin 16, 95, 124, 127
  rich normality 29, 45
  empathy 33, 38–39, 53, 61, 78, 99, 102

chaos, chaotic 1, 6, 14, 22, 26–27, 36, 54–56, 100, 111, 120, 123, 130

clown 15, 95–103, 123–126, 128–129, 145–146

collective biography 1, 8–13, 74, 106

competition 3, 17, 35

curriculum 29, 43, 58, 62–64, 68, 91

D

DAC, Drama Action Centre 15, 89, 96

Dahlberg and Moss 4–5, 33, 91

Deleuze *1983* 47, 94
  1988 73
  1990 19, 142
  1994 46–47, 73
  1995 92, 100
  and Guattari *1987* 2–3, 8, 21, 24, 29, 50, 73, 78, 92, 94, 99–100, 135–136, 140, 145
  and Parnet *1987* 15, 92, 102
  and Parnet *2002* 46–47, 51

desire 2–4, 27–28, 59, 73, 94–99, 114, 136, 140, 142, 144

differenciation 13–20, 33–34, 45–53 88–89, 93, 143–148

E

Ellsworth 113, 114, 134

embodiment 72, 109, 147, 156

ethics 3, 13–14, 28–29, 33, 69, 74, 84, 87, 148

ethical encounter 14, 68, 74, 78, 84–88, 149

F

Foucault 29, 47, 90, 110, 112, 127, 129

G

Grosz 2, 55, 92, 133, 141
  art 2, 6, 26, 55, 103, 146–147
  difference 71, 138

H

haecceity 9, 23, 34, 46, 50, 58, 62

Hickey-Moody and Malins 2, 29, 59, 89, 99
  affect 11–12, 29
  bodies 70, 76, 93
  space 20–21, 45, 78

hundred languages 14, 33–34, 36, 39, 42, 51, 53

I

improvisation 90, 91, 93, 94

K

knowledge 6–10, 63–64, 81–82, 86, 117–118, 137–138, 142–145
  new 82, 122, 143
  professional 1, 60
  lack of 111, 129

L

LeCoq 15, 91, 92, 94, 96, 102

Lenz Taguchi 4–5

Levinas 14, 71, 72, 74, 78, 84, 88

line of flight 20–21, 86, 92, 99, 134, 143, 145
  child's 24–25, 54, 56–59, 62, 64

listening 8–11, 13, 29, 31–52, 60–61, 64–65, 77–78, 91, 93, 140, 142–143, 149

M

materiality 55, 63, 74, 103, 132, 138

INDEX

May 72

memory 9–11, 20–21, 96, 105–106, 116, 120, 124, 143
   individual and group 6, 135
   sensory 136

molar striations 25, 27, 36, 60 140

Moss 4, 5, 33, 91

mo(ve)ment 9–10, 78, 141

N

Nancy 6, 11, 64, 72, 121, 125, 141

neoliberal, neoliberalism 3–5, 16–17, 29, 63, 135, 148

normative 9, 23, 33, 95, 140
   classroom 36–37

not-yet-known 2, 12–13, 53, 64–65, 129, 141, 146

O

Oasis 13–14, 33–36, 40–46, 51–52

P

pedagogical encounter 12, 14, 69–74, 83–88, 132, 145–149

pedagogy, emergent 12, 55, 103

performance 3–4, 26, 64, 69, 72, 83, 85, 139
   gender 146
   LeCoq 91, 94, 102
   pedagogical 3, 70
   public 85, 91, 102, 145
   student 75–79, 89–90

places, pedagogical 2, 6

power 2–3, 10–11, 16, 27–29, 63, 142
   -lessness 27, 36, 131, 136, 138
   Bell 72, 82
   Deleuze 46, 72
   empowerment 63
   total 99
   transformative 93, 132

productivity 3

R

recognition 28, 34, 37–39, 46, 50, 70, 91, 100

Reggio Emilia 5–7, 11–14, 89, 91, 132–135, 143
   classroom 19, 133, 139

relationality 1, 4–5, 34–36, 42, 54–55, 60–68
   ethical 28–29, 74, 148

respect 34, 44–46, 60, 122
   for difference 11, 14, 39, 44–45, 53, 65, 78

responsibility 4–5, 66–67, 74, 82–87, 93–94

Rinaldi 3–4, 28, 42, 94, 108, 145
   hundred languages 14, 34
   listening 10, 93, 142

Rudd 4, 16, 84, 85, 87

S

schizophrenia 2–3

second skin 7–8, 95–96, 111–113, 127–134, 137–138, 141–144

psychic 7, *16*, 102, 124, 127–128, 133

space, affective 15, 76, 105

space, pedagogical 3, 8, 45, 64, 78, 81–82, 146

space, relational 11, 35, 53, 56, 64–65, 132, 139

Springgay 1–2, 55, 63, 98, 103, 107

Stivale 86

subject   *affective* 73
    individual/singular 7, 10, 16, 28–29, 64, 84–85
    rational 141
    teacher 1, 69, 82

subjectivity 5, 22, 74, 84

T

Todd 65, 71, 77–78, 84, 87–88, 94

transformation 1–2, 19, 63–66, 95, 97, 120, 139, 141

V

vulnerable, vulnerability 1, 4, 10, 63–65, 76–77, 122, 149

Y

Youdell 14, 36–39, 45–47

Yunupingu 85, 86

COMPLICATED CONVERSATION

A BOOK SERIES OF CURRICULUM STUDIES

Reframing the curricular challenge educators face after a decade of school deform, the books published in Peter Lang's Complicated Conversation Series testify to the ethical demands of our time, our place, our profession. What does it mean for us to teach now, in an era structured by political polarization, economic destabilization, and the prospect of climate catastrophe? Each of the books in the Complicated Conversation Series provides provocative paths, theoretical and practical, to a very different future. In this resounding series of scholarly and pedagogical interventions into the nightmare that is the present, we hear once again the sound of silence breaking, supporting us to rearticulate our pedagogical convictions in this time of terrorism, reframing curriculum as committed to the complicated conversation that is intercultural communication, self-understanding, and global justice.

The series editor is

    Dr. William F. Pinar
    Department of Curriculum Studies
    2125 Main Mall
    Faculty of Education
    University of British Columbia
    Vancouver, British Columbia V6T 1Z4
    CANADA

To order other books in this series, please contact our Customer Service Department:

    (800) 770-LANG (within the U.S.)
    (212) 647-7706 (outside the U.S.)
    (212) 647-7707 FAX

Or browse online by series:

    www.peterlang.com

www.ingramcontent.com/pod-product-compliance
Lightning Source LLC
Chambersburg PA
CBHW050551300426
44112CB00013B/1874